C-1263 CAREER EXAMINATION SERIES

This is your
PASSBOOK for...

EEG Technician

Test Preparation Study Guide
Questions & Answers

NATIONAL LEARNING CORPORATION®

COPYRIGHT NOTICE

This book is SOLELY intended for, is sold ONLY to, and its use is RESTRICTED to individual, bona fide applicants or candidates who qualify by virtue of having seriously filed applications for appropriate license, certificate, professional and/or promotional advancement, higher school matriculation, scholarship, or other legitimate requirements of education and/or governmental authorities.

This book is NOT intended for use, class instruction, tutoring, training, duplication, copying, reprinting, excerption, or adaptation, etc., by:

1) Other publishers
2) Proprietors and/or Instructors of "Coaching" and/or Preparatory Courses
3) Personnel and/or Training Divisions of commercial, industrial, and governmental organizations
4) Schools, colleges, or universities and/or their departments and staffs, including teachers and other personnel
5) Testing Agencies or Bureaus
6) Study groups which seek by the purchase of a single volume to copy and/or duplicate and/or adapt this material for use by the group as a whole without having purchased individual volumes for each of the members of the group
7) Et al.

Such persons would be in violation of appropriate Federal and State statutes.

PROVISION OF LICENSING AGREEMENTS – Recognized educational, commercial, industrial, and governmental institutions and organizations, and others legitimately engaged in educational pursuits, including training, testing, and measurement activities, may address request for a licensing agreement to the copyright owners, who will determine whether, and under what conditions, including fees and charges, the materials in this book may be used them. In other words, a licensing facility exists for the legitimate use of the material in this book on other than an individual basis. However, it is asseverated and affirmed here that the material in this book CANNOT be used without the receipt of the express permission of such a licensing agreement from the Publishers. Inquiries re licensing should be addressed to the company, attention rights and permissions department.

All rights reserved, including the right of reproduction in whole or in part, in any form or by any means, electronic or mechanical, including photocopying, recording, or by any information storage and retrieval system, without permission in writing from the Publisher.

Copyright © 2024 by
National Learning Corporation

212 Michael Drive, Syosset, NY 11791
(516) 921-8888 • www.passbooks.com
E-mail: info@passbooks.com

PUBLISHED IN THE UNITED STATES OF AMERICA

PASSBOOK® SERIES

THE *PASSBOOK® SERIES* has been created to prepare applicants and candidates for the ultimate academic battlefield – the examination room.

At some time in our lives, each and every one of us may be required to take an examination – for validation, matriculation, admission, qualification, registration, certification, or licensure.

Based on the assumption that every applicant or candidate has met the basic formal educational standards, has taken the required number of courses, and read the necessary texts, the *PASSBOOK® SERIES* furnishes the one special preparation which may assure passing with confidence, instead of failing with insecurity. Examination questions – together with answers – are furnished as the basic vehicle for study so that the mysteries of the examination and its compounding difficulties may be eliminated or diminished by a sure method.

This book is meant to help you pass your examination provided that you qualify and are serious in your objective.

The entire field is reviewed through the huge store of content information which is succinctly presented through a provocative and challenging approach – the question-and-answer method.

A climate of success is established by furnishing the correct answers at the end of each test.

You soon learn to recognize types of questions, forms of questions, and patterns of questioning. You may even begin to anticipate expected outcomes.

You perceive that many questions are repeated or adapted so that you can gain acute insights, which may enable you to score many sure points.

You learn how to confront new questions, or types of questions, and to attack them confidently and work out the correct answers.

You note objectives and emphases, and recognize pitfalls and dangers, so that you may make positive educational adjustments.

Moreover, you are kept fully informed in relation to new concepts, methods, practices, and directions in the field.

You discover that you are actually taking the examination all the time: you are preparing for the examination by "taking" an examination, not by reading extraneous and/or supererogatory textbooks.

In short, this PASSBOOK®, used directedly, should be an important factor in helping you to pass your test.

EEG TECHNICIAN

DUTIES

Electroencephalograph Technicians prepare and posture patients to make electroencephalograms and observe and record all artifacts and clinical symptoms. They make minor repairs to the machine and are responsible for maintaining records of supplies. They may also be called upon to assist with, or give practical demonstrations of, the operation of an electroencephalograph to students, trainees, or hospital or clinical personnel. Work is performed under the supervision of a psychiatrist, neurologist, or other medical officer.

SUBJECT OF EXAMINATION

Written test designed to test for knowledge, skills, and/or abilities in such areas as:
1. The operation and construction of an electroencephalograph machine;
2. Techniques involved in taking electroencephalograms; and
3. Anatomy and terminology related to electroencephalography.

ELECTROENCEPHALOGRAPHIC TECHNICIANS

NATURE OF THE WORK

EEG (electroencephalographic) technicians fulfill an important function in the diagnosis of brain disease and infections through electroencephalograph - a system which records in graphic form the electrical activity of the brain.

Neurologists and other qualified professionals use EEG's to help diagnose such brain disorders as epilepsy and tumors, and assess damage and recovery· after cerebral vascular strokes. Use of EEG's in pinpointing the time brain functions stop has also made them very important in vital organ transplant operations.

To carry out the procedure, the *BEG* technician measures the patient's head and attaches electrodes leading from the electroencephalograph to the patient's head. The complex machine detects and graphs (EEG's) the electrical activity of the patient's brain. Interpretation of the electroencephalograms is done by professional EEG personnel, often neurologists. However, the EEG technician must have some knowledge of medicine, anatomy, and physiology to understand the condition of the patient.

EEG technicians make routine repairs and replacements to keep equipment in good working order. They also schedule appointments and keep records of services performed for patients.

PLACES OF EMPLOYMENT

About 20,000 persons work as electroencephalograph technicians. Although EEG technicians work primarily in the neurology department of hospitals, some work in neurologists' offices.

TRAINING, OTHER QUALIFICATIONS, AND ADVANCEMENT

Most EEG technicians were trained on the job by experienced EEG personnel. However, with advances in medical technology, electroencephalograph equipment becomes increasingly more sophisticated and requires technicians with more training.

About 10 programs in colleges and medical schools trained EEG technicians. These programs lasted for 6 months to one year.

In recognition of the need for educational programs for EEG technicians, the Council on Medical Education of the American Medical Association, in collaboration with the American Electroencephalographic Society, the American Medical Electroencephalographic Association and the American Society of Electroencephalographic Technologists, developed a set of standards for use in the establishment of educational programs for EEG technicians and technologists. These standards recommend that programs last from 6 months to one year and include laboratory experience as well as classroom instruction in anatomy, physiology, neurophysiology. clinical and internal medicine, psychiatry, and electronics and instrumentation. Programs may be carried on in colleges, junior colleges, medical schools, hospitals, vocational or technical schools. In 1973, these standards were adopted by the American Medication Association's House of Delegates.

EEG technicians who have one year of training and a year of experience, and successfully complete a written and oral examination administered by the American Board of Registration of Electroencephalograph Technologists (ABRET), may become registered (R.EEG.T.). Although not a general requirement for employment, registration by ABRET is acknowledgment of a technician's qualifications, and makes better-paying jobs easier to obtain.

People who want to enter this field should have manual dexterity, good vision, an aptitude for working with electronic equipment, and the ability to work with patients and with other members of the hospital team.

As openings occur, some EEG technicians in large hospitals advance to chief EEG technician and have increased responsibilities in laboratory management and in teaching basic techniques to new personnel. Chief EEG technicians are supervised by an electroencephalographer, or a neurologist or neurosurgeon.

EMPLOYMENT OUTLOOK

Employment opportunities for EEG technicians are expected to be very good through the late-2010s. The occupation is expected to grow rapidly because of increased use of EEG's in the diagnosis and monitoring of patients with brain disease and during surgical procedures. Factors contributing to the overall increase in health services, such as expanding population and rising living standards, also will stimulate the need for EEG technicians.

In addition to openings that will result from growth of the occupation, many will arise because of the need to replace the large number of workers who retire or leave the field for other reasons.

WORKING CONDITIONS

EEG technicians in hospitals receive the same benefits as other hospital personnel, including hospitalization, vacation, and sick leave. Some institutions may provide tuition assistance or free courses, pension programs, uniforms, and parking.

EEG technicians generally work a 40-hour week with little afterhours or Saturday work involved.

SOURCES OF ADDITIONAL INFORMATION

Local hospitals can supply information about employment opportunities. Additional information about the work of EEG technicians is available from:

American Hospital Association

One North Franklin, Chicago, IL 60606

For information on registration, contact:

American Board of Registration of Electroencephalographic Technologists

2509 West Iles Ave., Suite 102, Springfield, IL 62704

HOW TO TAKE A TEST

I. YOU MUST PASS AN EXAMINATION

A. *WHAT EVERY CANDIDATE SHOULD KNOW*

Examination applicants often ask us for help in preparing for the written test. What can I study in advance? What kinds of questions will be asked? How will the test be given? How will the papers be graded?

As an applicant for a civil service examination, you may be wondering about some of these things. Our purpose here is to suggest effective methods of advance study and to describe civil service examinations.

Your chances for success on this examination can be increased if you know how to prepare. Those "pre-examination jitters" can be reduced if you know what to expect. You can even experience an adventure in good citizenship if you know why civil service exams are given.

B. *WHY ARE CIVIL SERVICE EXAMINATIONS GIVEN?*

Civil service examinations are important to you in two ways. As a citizen, you want public jobs filled by employees who know how to do their work. As a job seeker, you want a fair chance to compete for that job on an equal footing with other candidates. The best-known means of accomplishing this two-fold goal is the competitive examination.

Exams are widely publicized throughout the nation. They may be administered for jobs in federal, state, city, municipal, town or village governments or agencies.

Any citizen may apply, with some limitations, such as the age or residence of applicants. Your experience and education may be reviewed to see whether you meet the requirements for the particular examination. When these requirements exist, they are reasonable and applied consistently to all applicants. Thus, a competitive examination may cause you some uneasiness now, but it is your privilege and safeguard.

C. *HOW ARE CIVIL SERVICE EXAMS DEVELOPED?*

Examinations are carefully written by trained technicians who are specialists in the field known as "psychological measurement," in consultation with recognized authorities in the field of work that the test will cover. These experts recommend the subject matter areas or skills to be tested; only those knowledges or skills important to your success on the job are included. The most reliable books and source materials available are used as references. Together, the experts and technicians judge the difficulty level of the questions.

Test technicians know how to phrase questions so that the problem is clearly stated. Their ethics do not permit "trick" or "catch" questions. Questions may have been tried out on sample groups, or subjected to statistical analysis, to determine their usefulness.

Written tests are often used in combination with performance tests, ratings of training and experience, and oral interviews. All of these measures combine to form the best-known means of finding the right person for the right job.

II. HOW TO PASS THE WRITTEN TEST

A. NATURE OF THE EXAMINATION

To prepare intelligently for civil service examinations, you should know how they differ from school examinations you have taken. In school you were assigned certain definite pages to read or subjects to cover. The examination questions were quite detailed and usually emphasized memory. Civil service exams, on the other hand, try to discover your present ability to perform the duties of a position, plus your potentiality to learn these duties. In other words, a civil service exam attempts to predict how successful you will be. Questions cover such a broad area that they cannot be as minute and detailed as school exam questions.

In the public service similar kinds of work, or positions, are grouped together in one "class." This process is known as *position-classification*. All the positions in a class are paid according to the salary range for that class. One class title covers all of these positions, and they are all tested by the same examination.

B. FOUR BASIC STEPS

1) Study the announcement

How, then, can you know what subjects to study? Our best answer is: "Learn as much as possible about the class of positions for which you've applied." The exam will test the knowledge, skills and abilities needed to do the work.

Your most valuable source of information about the position you want is the official exam announcement. This announcement lists the training and experience qualifications. Check these standards and apply only if you come reasonably close to meeting them.

The brief description of the position in the examination announcement offers some clues to the subjects which will be tested. Think about the job itself. Review the duties in your mind. Can you perform them, or are there some in which you are rusty? Fill in the blank spots in your preparation.

Many jurisdictions preview the written test in the exam announcement by including a section called "Knowledge and Abilities Required," "Scope of the Examination," or some similar heading. Here you will find out specifically what fields will be tested.

2) Review your own background

Once you learn in general what the position is all about, and what you need to know to do the work, ask yourself which subjects you already know fairly well and which need improvement. You may wonder whether to concentrate on improving your strong areas or on building some background in your fields of weakness. When the announcement has specified "some knowledge" or "considerable knowledge," or has used adjectives like "beginning principles of..." or "advanced ... methods," you can get a clue as to the number and difficulty of questions to be asked in any given field. More questions, and hence broader coverage, would be included for those subjects which are more important in the work. Now weigh your strengths and weaknesses against the job requirements and prepare accordingly.

3) Determine the level of the position

Another way to tell how intensively you should prepare is to understand the level of the job for which you are applying. Is it the entering level? In other words, is this the position in which beginners in a field of work are hired? Or is it an intermediate or advanced level? Sometimes this is indicated by such words as "Junior" or "Senior" in the class title. Other jurisdictions use Roman numerals to designate the level – Clerk I, Clerk II, for example. The word "Supervisor" sometimes appears in the title. If the level is not indicated by the title, check the description of duties. Will you be working under very close supervision, or will you have responsibility for independent decisions in this work?

4) Choose appropriate study materials

Now that you know the subjects to be examined and the relative amount of each subject to be covered, you can choose suitable study materials. For beginning level jobs, or even advanced ones, if you have a pronounced weakness in some aspect of your training, read a modern, standard textbook in that field. Be sure it is up to date and has general coverage. Such books are normally available at your library, and the librarian will be glad to help you locate one. For entry-level positions, questions of appropriate difficulty are chosen – neither highly advanced questions, nor those too simple. Such questions require careful thought but not advanced training.

If the position for which you are applying is technical or advanced, you will read more advanced, specialized material. If you are already familiar with the basic principles of your field, elementary textbooks would waste your time. Concentrate on advanced textbooks and technical periodicals. Think through the concepts and review difficult problems in your field.

These are all general sources. You can get more ideas on your own initiative, following these leads. For example, training manuals and publications of the government agency which employs workers in your field can be useful, particularly for technical and professional positions. A letter or visit to the government department involved may result in more specific study suggestions, and certainly will provide you with a more definite idea of the exact nature of the position you are seeking.

III. KINDS OF TESTS

Tests are used for purposes other than measuring knowledge and ability to perform specified duties. For some positions, it is equally important to test ability to make adjustments to new situations or to profit from training. In others, basic mental abilities not dependent on information are essential. Questions which test these things may not appear as pertinent to the duties of the position as those which test for knowledge and information. Yet they are often highly important parts of a fair examination. For very general questions, it is almost impossible to help you direct your study efforts. What we can do is to point out some of the more common of these general abilities needed in public service positions and describe some typical questions.

1) General information

Broad, general information has been found useful for predicting job success in some kinds of work. This is tested in a variety of ways, from vocabulary lists to questions about current events. Basic background in some field of work, such as sociology or economics, may be sampled in a group of questions. Often these are principles which have become familiar to most persons through exposure rather than through formal training. It is difficult to advise you how to study for these questions; being alert to the world around you is our best suggestion.

2) Verbal ability

An example of an ability needed in many positions is verbal or language ability. Verbal ability is, in brief, the ability to use and understand words. Vocabulary and grammar tests are typical measures of this ability. Reading comprehension or paragraph interpretation questions are common in many kinds of civil service tests. You are given a paragraph of written material and asked to find its central meaning.

3) Numerical ability
Number skills can be tested by the familiar arithmetic problem, by checking paired lists of numbers to see which are alike and which are different, or by interpreting charts and graphs. In the latter test, a graph may be printed in the test booklet which you are asked to use as the basis for answering questions.

4) Observation
A popular test for law-enforcement positions is the observation test. A picture is shown to you for several minutes, then taken away. Questions about the picture test your ability to observe both details and larger elements.

5) Following directions
In many positions in the public service, the employee must be able to carry out written instructions dependably and accurately. You may be given a chart with several columns, each column listing a variety of information. The questions require you to carry out directions involving the information given in the chart.

6) Skills and aptitudes
Performance tests effectively measure some manual skills and aptitudes. When the skill is one in which you are trained, such as typing or shorthand, you can practice. These tests are often very much like those given in business school or high school courses. For many of the other skills and aptitudes, however, no short-time preparation can be made. Skills and abilities natural to you or that you have developed throughout your lifetime are being tested.

Many of the general questions just described provide all the data needed to answer the questions and ask you to use your reasoning ability to find the answers. Your best preparation for these tests, as well as for tests of facts and ideas, is to be at your physical and mental best. You, no doubt, have your own methods of getting into an exam-taking mood and keeping "in shape." The next section lists some ideas on this subject.

IV. KINDS OF QUESTIONS

Only rarely is the "essay" question, which you answer in narrative form, used in civil service tests. Civil service tests are usually of the short-answer type. Full instructions for answering these questions will be given to you at the examination. But in case this is your first experience with short-answer questions and separate answer sheets, here is what you need to know:

1) Multiple-choice Questions
Most popular of the short-answer questions is the "multiple choice" or "best answer" question. It can be used, for example, to test for factual knowledge, ability to solve problems or judgment in meeting situations found at work.
A multiple-choice question is normally one of three types—
- It can begin with an incomplete statement followed by several possible endings. You are to find the one ending which *best* completes the statement, although some of the others may not be entirely wrong.
- It can also be a complete statement in the form of a question which is answered by choosing one of the statements listed.

- It can be in the form of a problem – again you select the best answer.

Here is an example of a multiple-choice question with a discussion which should give you some clues as to the method for choosing the right answer:

When an employee has a complaint about his assignment, the action which will *best* help him overcome his difficulty is to
   A. discuss his difficulty with his coworkers
   B. take the problem to the head of the organization
   C. take the problem to the person who gave him the assignment
   D. say nothing to anyone about his complaint

In answering this question, you should study each of the choices to find which is best. Consider choice "A" – Certainly an employee may discuss his complaint with fellow employees, but no change or improvement can result, and the complaint remains unresolved. Choice "B" is a poor choice since the head of the organization probably does not know what assignment you have been given, and taking your problem to him is known as "going over the head" of the supervisor. The supervisor, or person who made the assignment, is the person who can clarify it or correct any injustice. Choice "C" is, therefore, correct. To say nothing, as in choice "D," is unwise. Supervisors have and interest in knowing the problems employees are facing, and the employee is seeking a solution to his problem.

2) True/False Questions

The "true/false" or "right/wrong" form of question is sometimes used. Here a complete statement is given. Your job is to decide whether the statement is right or wrong.

SAMPLE: A roaming cell-phone call to a nearby city costs less than a non-roaming call to a distant city.

This statement is wrong, or false, since roaming calls are more expensive.

This is not a complete list of all possible question forms, although most of the others are variations of these common types. You will always get complete directions for answering questions. Be sure you understand *how* to mark your answers – ask questions until you do.

V. RECORDING YOUR ANSWERS

Computer terminals are used more and more today for many different kinds of exams.
For an examination with very few applicants, you may be told to record your answers in the test booklet itself. Separate answer sheets are much more common. If this separate answer sheet is to be scored by machine – and this is often the case – it is highly important that you mark your answers correctly in order to get credit.
An electronic scoring machine is often used in civil service offices because of the speed with which papers can be scored. Machine-scored answer sheets must be marked with a pencil, which will be given to you. This pencil has a high graphite content which responds to the electronic scoring machine. As a matter of fact, stray dots may register as answers, so do not let your pencil rest on the answer sheet while you are pondering the correct answer. Also, if your pencil lead breaks or is otherwise defective, ask for another.

Since the answer sheet will be dropped in a slot in the scoring machine, be careful not to bend the corners or get the paper crumpled.

The answer sheet normally has five vertical columns of numbers, with 30 numbers to a column. These numbers correspond to the question numbers in your test booklet. After each number, going across the page are four or five pairs of dotted lines. These short dotted lines have small letters or numbers above them. The first two pairs may also have a "T" or "F" above the letters. This indicates that the first two pairs only are to be used if the questions are of the true-false type. If the questions are multiple choice, disregard the "T" and "F" and pay attention only to the small letters or numbers.

Answer your questions in the manner of the sample that follows:

32. The largest city in the United States is
    A. Washington, D.C.
    B. New York City
    C. Chicago
    D. Detroit
    E. San Francisco

1) Choose the answer you think is best. (New York City is the largest, so "B" is correct.)
2) Find the row of dotted lines numbered the same as the question you are answering. (Find row number 32)
3) Find the pair of dotted lines corresponding to the answer. (Find the pair of lines under the mark "B.")
4) Make a solid black mark between the dotted lines.

VI. BEFORE THE TEST

Common sense will help you find procedures to follow to get ready for an examination. Too many of us, however, overlook these sensible measures. Indeed, nervousness and fatigue have been found to be the most serious reasons why applicants fail to do their best on civil service tests. Here is a list of reminders:

- Begin your preparation early – Don't wait until the last minute to go scurrying around for books and materials or to find out what the position is all about.
- Prepare continuously – An hour a night for a week is better than an all-night cram session. This has been definitely established. What is more, a night a week for a month will return better dividends than crowding your study into a shorter period of time.
- Locate the place of the exam – You have been sent a notice telling you when and where to report for the examination. If the location is in a different town or otherwise unfamiliar to you, it would be well to inquire the best route and learn something about the building.
- Relax the night before the test – Allow your mind to rest. Do not study at all that night. Plan some mild recreation or diversion; then go to bed early and get a good night's sleep.
- Get up early enough to make a leisurely trip to the place for the test – This way unforeseen events, traffic snarls, unfamiliar buildings, etc. will not upset you.
- Dress comfortably – A written test is not a fashion show. You will be known by number and not by name, so wear something comfortable.

- Leave excess paraphernalia at home – Shopping bags and odd bundles will get in your way. You need bring only the items mentioned in the official notice you received; usually everything you need is provided. Do not bring reference books to the exam. They will only confuse those last minutes and be taken away from you when in the test room.
- Arrive somewhat ahead of time – If because of transportation schedules you must get there very early, bring a newspaper or magazine to take your mind off yourself while waiting.
- Locate the examination room – When you have found the proper room, you will be directed to the seat or part of the room where you will sit. Sometimes you are given a sheet of instructions to read while you are waiting. Do not fill out any forms until you are told to do so; just read them and be prepared.
- Relax and prepare to listen to the instructions
- If you have any physical problem that may keep you from doing your best, be sure to tell the test administrator. If you are sick or in poor health, you really cannot do your best on the exam. You can come back and take the test some other time.

VII. AT THE TEST

The day of the test is here and you have the test booklet in your hand. The temptation to get going is very strong. Caution! There is more to success than knowing the right answers. You must know how to identify your papers and understand variations in the type of short-answer question used in this particular examination. Follow these suggestions for maximum results from your efforts:

1) Cooperate with the monitor

The test administrator has a duty to create a situation in which you can be as much at ease as possible. He will give instructions, tell you when to begin, check to see that you are marking your answer sheet correctly, and so on. He is not there to guard you, although he will see that your competitors do not take unfair advantage. He wants to help you do your best.

2) Listen to all instructions

Don't jump the gun! Wait until you understand all directions. In most civil service tests you get more time than you need to answer the questions. So don't be in a hurry. Read each word of instructions until you clearly understand the meaning. Study the examples, listen to all announcements and follow directions. Ask questions if you do not understand what to do.

3) Identify your papers

Civil service exams are usually identified by number only. You will be assigned a number; you must not put your name on your test papers. Be sure to copy your number correctly. Since more than one exam may be given, copy your exact examination title.

4) Plan your time

Unless you are told that a test is a "speed" or "rate of work" test, speed itself is usually not important. Time enough to answer all the questions will be provided, but this does not mean that you have all day. An overall time limit has been set. Divide the total time (in minutes) by the number of questions to determine the approximate time you have for each question.

5) Do not linger over difficult questions

If you come across a difficult question, mark it with a paper clip (useful to have along) and come back to it when you have been through the booklet. One caution if you do this – be sure to skip a number on your answer sheet as well. Check often to be sure that you have not lost your place and that you are marking in the row numbered the same as the question you are answering.

6) Read the questions

Be sure you know what the question asks! Many capable people are unsuccessful because they failed to *read* the questions correctly.

7) Answer all questions

Unless you have been instructed that a penalty will be deducted for incorrect answers, it is better to guess than to omit a question.

8) Speed tests

It is often better NOT to guess on speed tests. It has been found that on timed tests people are tempted to spend the last few seconds before time is called in marking answers at random – without even reading them – in the hope of picking up a few extra points. To discourage this practice, the instructions may warn you that your score will be "corrected" for guessing. That is, a penalty will be applied. The incorrect answers will be deducted from the correct ones, or some other penalty formula will be used.

9) Review your answers

If you finish before time is called, go back to the questions you guessed or omitted to give them further thought. Review other answers if you have time.

10) Return your test materials

If you are ready to leave before others have finished or time is called, take ALL your materials to the monitor and leave quietly. Never take any test material with you. The monitor can discover whose papers are not complete, and taking a test booklet may be grounds for disqualification.

VIII. EXAMINATION TECHNIQUES

1) Read the general instructions carefully. These are usually printed on the first page of the exam booklet. As a rule, these instructions refer to the timing of the examination; the fact that you should not start work until the signal and must stop work at a signal, etc. If there are any *special* instructions, such as a choice of questions to be answered, make sure that you note this instruction carefully.

2) When you are ready to start work on the examination, that is as soon as the signal has been given, read the instructions to each question booklet, underline any key words or phrases, such as *least, best, outline, describe* and the like. In this way you will tend to answer as requested rather than discover on reviewing your paper that you *listed without describing*, that you selected the *worst* choice rather than the *best* choice, etc.

3) If the examination is of the objective or multiple-choice type – that is, each question will also give a series of possible answers: A, B, C or D, and you are called upon to select the best answer and write the letter next to that answer on your answer paper – it is advisable to start answering each question in turn. There may be anywhere from 50 to 100 such questions in the three or four hours allotted and you can see how much time would be taken if you read through all the questions before beginning to answer any. Furthermore, if you come across a question or group of questions which you know would be difficult to answer, it would undoubtedly affect your handling of all the other questions.

4) If the examination is of the essay type and contains but a few questions, it is a moot point as to whether you should read all the questions before starting to answer any one. Of course, if you are given a choice – say five out of seven and the like – then it is essential to read all the questions so you can eliminate the two that are most difficult. If, however, you are asked to answer all the questions, there may be danger in trying to answer the easiest one first because you may find that you will spend too much time on it. The best technique is to answer the first question, then proceed to the second, etc.

5) Time your answers. Before the exam begins, write down the time it started, then add the time allowed for the examination and write down the time it must be completed, then divide the time available somewhat as follows:
    - If 3-1/2 hours are allowed, that would be 210 minutes. If you have 80 objective-type questions, that would be an average of 2-1/2 minutes per question. Allow yourself no more than 2 minutes per question, or a total of 160 minutes, which will permit about 50 minutes to review.
    - If for the time allotment of 210 minutes there are 7 essay questions to answer, that would average about 30 minutes a question. Give yourself only 25 minutes per question so that you have about 35 minutes to review.

6) The most important instruction is to *read each question* and make sure you know what is wanted. The second most important instruction is to *time yourself properly* so that you answer every question. The third most important instruction is to *answer every question*. Guess if you have to but include something for each question. Remember that you will receive no credit for a blank and will probably receive some credit if you write something in answer to an essay question. If you guess a letter – say "B" for a multiple-choice question – you may have guessed right. If you leave a blank as an answer to a multiple-choice question, the examiners may respect your feelings but it will not add a point to your score. Some exams may penalize you for wrong answers, so in such cases *only*, you may not want to guess unless you have some basis for your answer.

7) Suggestions
    a. Objective-type questions
        1. Examine the question booklet for proper sequence of pages and questions
        2. Read all instructions carefully
        3. Skip any question which seems too difficult; return to it after all other questions have been answered
        4. Apportion your time properly; do not spend too much time on any single question or group of questions

5. Note and underline key words – *all, most, fewest, least, best, worst, same, opposite*, etc.
6. Pay particular attention to negatives
7. Note unusual option, e.g., unduly long, short, complex, different or similar in content to the body of the question
8. Observe the use of "hedging" words – *probably, may, most likely*, etc.
9. Make sure that your answer is put next to the same number as the question
10. Do not second-guess unless you have good reason to believe the second answer is definitely more correct
11. Cross out original answer if you decide another answer is more accurate; do not erase until you are ready to hand your paper in
12. Answer all questions; guess unless instructed otherwise
13. Leave time for review

  b. Essay questions
   1. Read each question carefully
   2. Determine exactly what is wanted. Underline key words or phrases.
   3. Decide on outline or paragraph answer
   4. Include many different points and elements unless asked to develop any one or two points or elements
   5. Show impartiality by giving pros and cons unless directed to select one side only
   6. Make and write down any assumptions you find necessary to answer the questions
   7. Watch your English, grammar, punctuation and choice of words
   8. Time your answers; don't crowd material

8) Answering the essay question

Most essay questions can be answered by framing the specific response around several key words or ideas. Here are a few such key words or ideas:

M's: manpower, materials, methods, money, management
P's: purpose, program, policy, plan, procedure, practice, problems, pitfalls, personnel, public relations

  a. Six basic steps in handling problems:
   1. Preliminary plan and background development
   2. Collect information, data and facts
   3. Analyze and interpret information, data and facts
   4. Analyze and develop solutions as well as make recommendations
   5. Prepare report and sell recommendations
   6. Install recommendations and follow up effectiveness

  b. Pitfalls to avoid
   1. *Taking things for granted* – A statement of the situation does not necessarily imply that each of the elements is necessarily true; for example, a complaint may be invalid and biased so that all that can be taken for granted is that a complaint has been registered

2. *Considering only one side of a situation* – Wherever possible, indicate several alternatives and then point out the reasons you selected the best one
3. *Failing to indicate follow up* – Whenever your answer indicates action on your part, make certain that you will take proper follow-up action to see how successful your recommendations, procedures or actions turn out to be
4. *Taking too long in answering any single question* – Remember to time your answers properly

IX. AFTER THE TEST

Scoring procedures differ in detail among civil service jurisdictions although the general principles are the same. Whether the papers are hand-scored or graded by machine we have described, they are nearly always graded by number. That is, the person who marks the paper knows only the number – never the name – of the applicant. Not until all the papers have been graded will they be matched with names. If other tests, such as training and experience or oral interview ratings have been given, scores will be combined. Different parts of the examination usually have different weights. For example, the written test might count 60 percent of the final grade, and a rating of training and experience 40 percent. In many jurisdictions, veterans will have a certain number of points added to their grades.

After the final grade has been determined, the names are placed in grade order and an eligible list is established. There are various methods for resolving ties between those who get the same final grade – probably the most common is to place first the name of the person whose application was received first. Job offers are made from the eligible list in the order the names appear on it. You will be notified of your grade and your rank as soon as all these computations have been made. This will be done as rapidly as possible.

People who are found to meet the requirements in the announcement are called "eligibles." Their names are put on a list of eligible candidates. An eligible's chances of getting a job depend on how high he stands on this list and how fast agencies are filling jobs from the list.

When a job is to be filled from a list of eligibles, the agency asks for the names of people on the list of eligibles for that job. When the civil service commission receives this request, it sends to the agency the names of the three people highest on this list. Or, if the job to be filled has specialized requirements, the office sends the agency the names of the top three persons who meet these requirements from the general list.

The appointing officer makes a choice from among the three people whose names were sent to him. If the selected person accepts the appointment, the names of the others are put back on the list to be considered for future openings.

That is the rule in hiring from all kinds of eligible lists, whether they are for typist, carpenter, chemist, or something else. For every vacancy, the appointing officer has his choice of any one of the top three eligibles on the list. This explains why the person whose name is on top of the list sometimes does not get an appointment when some of the persons lower on the list do. If the appointing officer chooses the second or third eligible, the No. 1 eligible does not get a job at once, but stays on the list until he is appointed or the list is terminated.

X. HOW TO PASS THE INTERVIEW TEST

The examination for which you applied requires an oral interview test. You have already taken the written test and you are now being called for the interview test – the final part of the formal examination.

You may think that it is not possible to prepare for an interview test and that there are no procedures to follow during an interview. Our purpose is to point out some things you can do in advance that will help you and some good rules to follow and pitfalls to avoid while you are being interviewed.

What is an interview supposed to test?

The written examination is designed to test the technical knowledge and competence of the candidate; the oral is designed to evaluate intangible qualities, not readily measured otherwise, and to establish a list showing the relative fitness of each candidate – as measured against his competitors – for the position sought. Scoring is not on the basis of "right" and "wrong," but on a sliding scale of values ranging from "not passable" to "outstanding." As a matter of fact, it is possible to achieve a relatively low score without a single "incorrect" answer because of evident weakness in the qualities being measured.

Occasionally, an examination may consist entirely of an oral test – either an individual or a group oral. In such cases, information is sought concerning the technical knowledges and abilities of the candidate, since there has been no written examination for this purpose. More commonly, however, an oral test is used to supplement a written examination.

Who conducts interviews?

The composition of oral boards varies among different jurisdictions. In nearly all, a representative of the personnel department serves as chairman. One of the members of the board may be a representative of the department in which the candidate would work. In some cases, "outside experts" are used, and, frequently, a businessman or some other representative of the general public is asked to serve. Labor and management or other special groups may be represented. The aim is to secure the services of experts in the appropriate field.

However the board is composed, it is a good idea (and not at all improper or unethical) to ascertain in advance of the interview who the members are and what groups they represent. When you are introduced to them, you will have some idea of their backgrounds and interests, and at least you will not stutter and stammer over their names.

What should be done before the interview?

While knowledge about the board members is useful and takes some of the surprise element out of the interview, there is other preparation which is more substantive. It *is* possible to prepare for an oral interview – in several ways:

1) Keep a copy of your application and review it carefully before the interview

This may be the only document before the oral board, and the starting point of the interview. Know what education and experience you have listed there, and the sequence and dates of all of it. Sometimes the board will ask you to review the highlights of your experience for them; you should not have to hem and haw doing it.

2) Study the class specification and the examination announcement

Usually, the oral board has one or both of these to guide them. The qualities, characteristics or knowledges required by the position sought are stated in these documents. They offer valuable clues as to the nature of the oral interview. For example, if the job involves supervisory responsibilities, the announcement will usually indicate that knowledge of modern supervisory methods and the qualifications of the candidate as a supervisor will be tested. If so, you can expect such questions, frequently in the form of a hypothetical situation which you are expected to solve. NEVER go into an oral without knowledge of the duties and responsibilities of the job you seek.

3) Think through each qualification required

Try to visualize the kind of questions you would ask if you were a board member. How well could you answer them? Try especially to appraise your own knowledge and background in each area, *measured against the job sought*, and identify any areas in which you are weak. Be critical and realistic – do not flatter yourself.

4) Do some general reading in areas in which you feel you may be weak

For example, if the job involves supervision and your past experience has NOT, some general reading in supervisory methods and practices, particularly in the field of human relations, might be useful. Do NOT study agency procedures or detailed manuals. The oral board will be testing your understanding and capacity, not your memory.

5) Get a good night's sleep and watch your general health and mental attitude

You will want a clear head at the interview. Take care of a cold or any other minor ailment, and of course, no hangovers.

What should be done on the day of the interview?

Now comes the day of the interview itself. Give yourself plenty of time to get there. Plan to arrive somewhat ahead of the scheduled time, particularly if your appointment is in the fore part of the day. If a previous candidate fails to appear, the board might be ready for you a bit early. By early afternoon an oral board is almost invariably behind schedule if there are many candidates, and you may have to wait. Take along a book or magazine to read, or your application to review, but leave any extraneous material in the waiting room when you go in for your interview. In any event, relax and compose yourself.

The matter of dress is important. The board is forming impressions about you – from your experience, your manners, your attitude, and your appearance. Give your personal appearance careful attention. Dress your best, but not your flashiest. Choose conservative, appropriate clothing, and be sure it is immaculate. This is a business interview, and your appearance should indicate that you regard it as such. Besides, being well groomed and properly dressed will help boost your confidence.

Sooner or later, someone will call your name and escort you into the interview room. *This is it.* From here on you are on your own. It is too late for any more preparation. But remember, you asked for this opportunity to prove your fitness, and you are here because your request was granted.

What happens when you go in?

The usual sequence of events will be as follows: The clerk (who is often the board stenographer) will introduce you to the chairman of the oral board, who will introduce you to the other members of the board. Acknowledge the introductions before you sit down. Do not be surprised if you find a microphone facing you or a stenotypist sitting by. Oral interviews are usually recorded in the event of an appeal or other review.

Usually the chairman of the board will open the interview by reviewing the highlights of your education and work experience from your application – primarily for the benefit of the other members of the board, as well as to get the material into the record. Do not interrupt or comment unless there is an error or significant misinterpretation; if that is the case, do not hesitate. But do not quibble about insignificant matters. Also, he will usually ask you some question about your education, experience or your present job – partly to get you to start talking and to establish the interviewing "rapport." He may start the actual questioning, or turn it over to one of the other members. Frequently, each member undertakes the questioning on a particular area, one in which he is perhaps most competent, so you can expect each member to participate in the examination. Because time is limited, you may also expect some rather abrupt switches in the direction the questioning takes, so do not be upset by it. Normally, a board member will not pursue a single line of questioning unless he discovers a particular strength or weakness.

After each member has participated, the chairman will usually ask whether any member has any further questions, then will ask you if you have anything you wish to add. Unless you are expecting this question, it may floor you. Worse, it may start you off on an extended, extemporaneous speech. The board is not usually seeking more information. The question is principally to offer you a last opportunity to present further qualifications or to indicate that you have nothing to add. So, if you feel that a significant qualification or characteristic has been overlooked, it is proper to point it out in a sentence or so. Do not compliment the board on the thoroughness of their examination – they have been sketchy, and you know it. If you wish, merely say, "No thank you, I have nothing further to add." This is a point where you can "talk yourself out" of a good impression or fail to present an important bit of information. Remember, *you close the interview yourself.*

The chairman will then say, "That is all, Mr. _____, thank you." Do not be startled; the interview is over, and quicker than you think. Thank him, gather your belongings and take your leave. Save your sigh of relief for the other side of the door.

How to put your best foot forward

Throughout this entire process, you may feel that the board individually and collectively is trying to pierce your defenses, seek out your hidden weaknesses and embarrass and confuse you. Actually, this is not true. They are obliged to make an appraisal of your qualifications for the job you are seeking, and they want to see you in your best light. Remember, they must interview all candidates and a non-cooperative candidate may become a failure in spite of their best efforts to bring out his qualifications. Here are 15 suggestions that will help you:

1) Be natural – Keep your attitude confident, not cocky

If you are not confident that you can do the job, do not expect the board to be. Do not apologize for your weaknesses, try to bring out your strong points. The board is interested in a positive, not negative, presentation. Cockiness will antagonize any board member and make him wonder if you are covering up a weakness by a false show of strength.

2) Get comfortable, but don't lounge or sprawl

Sit erectly but not stiffly. A careless posture may lead the board to conclude that you are careless in other things, or at least that you are not impressed by the importance of the occasion. Either conclusion is natural, even if incorrect. Do not fuss with your clothing, a pencil or an ashtray. Your hands may occasionally be useful to emphasize a point; do not let them become a point of distraction.

3) Do not wisecrack or make small talk

This is a serious situation, and your attitude should show that you consider it as such. Further, the time of the board is limited – they do not want to waste it, and neither should you.

4) Do not exaggerate your experience or abilities
In the first place, from information in the application or other interviews and sources, the board may know more about you than you think. Secondly, you probably will not get away with it. An experienced board is rather adept at spotting such a situation, so do not take the chance.

5) If you know a board member, do not make a point of it, yet do not hide it
Certainly you are not fooling him, and probably not the other members of the board. Do not try to take advantage of your acquaintanceship – it will probably do you little good.

6) Do not dominate the interview
Let the board do that. They will give you the clues – do not assume that you have to do all the talking. Realize that the board has a number of questions to ask you, and do not try to take up all the interview time by showing off your extensive knowledge of the answer to the first one.

7) Be attentive
You only have 20 minutes or so, and you should keep your attention at its sharpest throughout. When a member is addressing a problem or question to you, give him your undivided attention. Address your reply principally to him, but do not exclude the other board members.

8) Do not interrupt
A board member may be stating a problem for you to analyze. He will ask you a question when the time comes. Let him state the problem, and wait for the question.

9) Make sure you understand the question
Do not try to answer until you are sure what the question is. If it is not clear, restate it in your own words or ask the board member to clarify it for you. However, do not haggle about minor elements.

10) Reply promptly but not hastily
A common entry on oral board rating sheets is "candidate responded readily," or "candidate hesitated in replies." Respond as promptly and quickly as you can, but do not jump to a hasty, ill-considered answer.

11) Do not be peremptory in your answers
A brief answer is proper – but do not fire your answer back. That is a losing game from your point of view. The board member can probably ask questions much faster than you can answer them.

12) Do not try to create the answer you think the board member wants
He is interested in what kind of mind you have and how it works – not in playing games. Furthermore, he can usually spot this practice and will actually grade you down on it.

13) Do not switch sides in your reply merely to agree with a board member
Frequently, a member will take a contrary position merely to draw you out and to see if you are willing and able to defend your point of view. Do not start a debate, yet do not surrender a good position. If a position is worth taking, it is worth defending.

14) Do not be afraid to admit an error in judgment if you are shown to be wrong

The board knows that you are forced to reply without any opportunity for careful consideration. Your answer may be demonstrably wrong. If so, admit it and get on with the interview.

15) Do not dwell at length on your present job

The opening question may relate to your present assignment. Answer the question but do not go into an extended discussion. You are being examined for a *new* job, not your present one. As a matter of fact, try to phrase ALL your answers in terms of the job for which you are being examined.

Basis of Rating

Probably you will forget most of these "do's" and "don'ts" when you walk into the oral interview room. Even remembering them all will not ensure you a passing grade. Perhaps you did not have the qualifications in the first place. But remembering them will help you to put your best foot forward, without treading on the toes of the board members.

Rumor and popular opinion to the contrary notwithstanding, an oral board wants you to make the best appearance possible. They know you are under pressure – but they also want to see how you respond to it as a guide to what your reaction would be under the pressures of the job you seek. They will be influenced by the degree of poise you display, the personal traits you show and the manner in which you respond.

ABOUT THIS BOOK

This book contains tests divided into Examination Sections. Go through each test, answering every question in the margin. We have also attached a sample answer sheet at the back of the book that can be removed and used. At the end of each test look at the answer key and check your answers. On the ones you got wrong, look at the right answer choice and learn. Do not fill in the answers first. Do not memorize the questions and answers, but understand the answer and principles involved. On your test, the questions will likely be different from the samples. Questions are changed and new ones added. If you understand these past questions you should have success with any changes that arise. Tests may consist of several types of questions. We have additional books on each subject should more study be advisable or necessary for you. Finally, the more you study, the better prepared you will be. This book is intended to be the last thing you study before you walk into the examination room. Prior study of relevant texts is also recommended. NLC publishes some of these in our Fundamental Series. Knowledge and good sense are important factors in passing your exam. Good luck also helps. So now study this Passbook, absorb the material contained within and take that knowledge into the examination. Then do your best to pass that exam.

EXAMINATION SECTION

EXAMINATION SECTION

TEST 1

DIRECTIONS: Each question or incomplete statement is followed by several suggested answers or completions. Select the one that BEST answers the question or completes the statement. *PRINT THE LETTER OF THE CORRECT ANSWER IN THE SPACE AT THE RIGHT.*

1. The chemical structure of a neuron is dependent on three major ions including all of the following EXCEPT
   A. magnesium B. potassium C. sodium D. chloride

    1.____

2. Which ion is found predominantly in extracellular fluid during the resting state of a neuron?
   A. Magnesium B. Potassium C. Sodium D. Chloride

    2.____

3. Which ion is found predominantly in intracellular fluid during the resting state of a neuron?
   A. Magnesium B. Potassium C. Sodium D. Chloride

    3.____

4. Cells in which an action potential can be triggered are considered to be
   A. excitable B. combustible C. susceptible D. irritable

    4.____

5. The approximate resting membrane potential of a neuron is _____ mV.
   A. -50 B. -60 C. -70 D. -80

    5.____

6. _____ is defined as a focal neurological deficit of sudden onset caused by central nervous system ischemia or hemorrhage.
   A. Cerebrovascular accident B. Transient ischemic attack
   C. Hemiparesis D. Hemiparesthesia

    6.____

7. Which of the following is the inability to perform a previously learned set of coordinated movements, not related to paralysis or lack of comprehension?
   A. Agnosia B. Apraxia C. Aphasia D. Dysphasia

    7.____

8. _____ is defined as difficulty naming an object or finding the desired words.
   A. Apraxia B. Aphasia C. Dysphasia D. Dysnomia

    8.____

9. Which of the following is a tumor that arises from the eighth cranial nerve and affects auditory and vestibular function often beginning in the internal auditory meatus and growing into the cerebellar pontine angle?
   A. Blastoma B. Glioma
   C. Meningioma D. Acoustic neuroma

    9.____

10. Which of the following is a common slow growing, almost always benign, brain tumor that arises from the pia-arachnoid cells and tends to occur near the falx in the parasagittal region and the sphenoid wing under the frontal region?
    A. Blastoma
    B. Glioma
    C. Meningioma
    D. Acoustic neuroma

10._____

11. Which cranial nerve is responsible for olfactory and sensor function?
    A. CN-1   B. CN-2   C. CN-3   D. CN-4

11._____

12. Which cranial nerve has sensory functions for the face and mouth and motor function for the muscles associated with mastication?
    A. CN-4   B. CN-5   C. CN-6   D. CN-7

12._____

13. The _____ nerve is responsible for sensations from internal organs or involuntary muscles such as the heart, stomach, intestines, throat, chest, and parasympathetic motor regulation of visceral organs.
    A. glossopharyngeal
    B. vagus
    C. vestibulocochlear
    D. hypoglossal

13._____

14. Which cranial nerves are associated with movements of the eye?
    A. 1, 2, and 3   B. 3, 4, and 6   C. 6, 7, and 9   D. 9, 10, and 12

14._____

15. Which part of the brain is responsible for voluntary movement, expressive language, social functioning, and short-term memory?
    A. Occipital lobe
    B. Parietal lobe
    C. Frontal lobe
    D. Cerebellum

15._____

16. Which are the main functions of the insula?
    A. Long term memory
    B. Balance/posture
    C. Emotional responses
    D. Taste sensations

16._____

17. In what area of the brain is the thalamus located?
    A. Cerebellum
    B. Insula
    C. Limbic system
    D. Diencephalon

17._____

18. What two ventricles are connected by the Aqueduct of Sylvius?
    A. 1st and 3rd B. 1st and 2nd C. 3rd and 4th D. 2nd and 4th

18._____

19. Cerebrospinal fluid is mainly produced by what structure?
    A. Choroid plexus
    B. Foramen of Munro
    C. Aqueduct of Sylvius
    D. Arachnoid Villi

19._____

20. The _____ artery supplies the insula, most of the lateral surface of the cerebral hemisphere, and the anterior tip of the temporal lobe.
    A. carotid
    B. anterior cerebral
    C. middle cerebral
    D. vertebral

20._____

21. Which structure makes collateral circulation to the brain possible due to a vascular anastomosis at the base of the brain?
    A. Choroid plexus
    B. Circle of Willis
    C. Aqueduct of Sylvius
    D. Arachnoid Villi

21.____

22. The right and left hemispheres are connected by the
    A. Choroid plexus
    B. Circle of Willis
    C. Corpus Callosum
    D. Arachnoid Villi

22.____

23. The _____ artery supplies blood to the anterior and middle cerebral arteries.
    A. internal carotid
    B. external carotid
    C. subclavian
    D. vertebral

23.____

24. A(n) _____ amplifier is an amplifier that amplifies only the difference in voltage between the two inputs. It does not amplify equal or common voltages at the two inputs.
    A. sequential
    B. differential
    C. potential
    D. exponential

24.____

25. The central sulcus, also known as the Rolandic fissure, is the boundary between what two lobes?
    A. Occipital and parietal
    B. Parietal and frontal
    C. Frontal and occipital
    D. Cerebellum and occipital

25.____

KEY (CORRECT ANSWERS)

1.	A	11.	A
2.	C	12.	B
3.	B	13.	B
4.	A	14.	B
5.	C	15.	C
6.	A	16.	D
7.	B	17.	D
8.	D	18.	C
9.	D	19.	A
10.	C	20.	C

21.	B
22.	C
23.	A
24.	B
25.	B

TEST 2

DIRECTIONS: Each question or incomplete statement is followed by several suggested answers or completions. Select the one that BEST answers the question or completes the statement. *PRINT THE LETTER OF THE CORRECT ANSWER IN THE SPACE AT THE RIGHT.*

1. _____ impedance is the impedance between components of the digital amplifier and not the impedance between the scalp of the electrode.
   A. Input   B. Output   C. Auxiliary   D. Accessory

   1._____

2. _____ is the ratio of output signal to input signal and it has no units of measure.
   A. Impedance   B. Gain   C. Amplifier   D. Sensitivity

   2._____

3. Which of the following is a combination of electronic components designed to increase voltage?
   A. Impedance   B. Gain   C. Amplifier   D. Sensitivity

   3._____

4. _____ is a measure of how much voltage is required to cause a deflection of a certain distance.
   A. Impedance   B. Gain   C. Amplifier   D. Sensitivity

   4._____

5. The _____ artery is a large vessel formed by the union of the two vertebral arteries.
   A. internal carotid   B. external carotid
   C. subclavian   D. basilar

   5._____

6. Which of the following is used to exclude waveforms that are out of range so that waveforms of most importance can be recorded without distortion?
   A. Filter   b. Gain   C. Amplifier   D. Sensitivity

   6._____

7. Which of the following is MOST attenuated by a time constant of 0.01 seconds?
   A. 0.3 Hz   B. 0.5 Hz   C. 3 Hz   D. 10 Hz

   7._____

8. Which filter setting will record the GREATEST amplitude of 0.4 Hz wave?
   A. 0.1 Hz   B. 0.3 Hz   C. 1 Hz   D. 5 Hz

   8._____

9. Which time constant will record the GREATEST amplitude of a 1 Hz wave?
   A. 0.03 seconds   B. 0.1 seconds   C. 0.1 Hz   D. 1 second

   9._____

10. Which should the common mode rejection be for a digital EEG instrument?
    A. 50dB   B. 60dB   C. 70dB   D. 80+dB

    10._____

11. The input impedance for a digital EEG instrument should be _____ megaohms.
    A. 7   B. 8   C. 9   D. 10+

    11._____

12. The sampling rate for a digital EEG instrument should be _____ Hz.
    A. 100-175   B. 250-400   C. 400-550   D. 550-700

13. Which of the following is defined as the number of digital points per second used to represent the analog signal?
    A. Sampling rate
    B. Nyquist frequency
    C. Input impedance
    D. Sensitivity

14. The _____, also known as the critical sampling rate, must be at least twice the fastest frequency.
    A. sampling rate
    B. Nyquist frequency
    C. input impedance
    D. sensitivity

15. _____ occurs when the ADC converter samples the analog signal at a rate less than two times its fastest frequency and the analog signal is then misinterpreted as a slower frequency waveform.
    A. Sampling   B. Sequencing   C. Aliasing   D. Biasing

16. Sharp waves or spikes in addition to slow waves, is the EEG finding MOST associated with which of the following?
    A. Cerebral hemorrhage
    B. Cerebrovascular accident
    C. Subdural hematoma
    D. Transient ischemic attack

17. If a patient has a CVA or TIA of vertebrobasilar origin, what lobes of the brain would show slow waves on an EEG?
    A. Frontal and parietal
    B. Parietal and temporal
    C. Temporal and occipital
    D. Frontal and occipital

18. The EEG strip shown above is indicative of what medical condition?
    A. Meningitis
    B. Cerebrovascular accident
    C. Subacute sclerosis pan encephalitis
    D. Hepatic encephalopathy

19.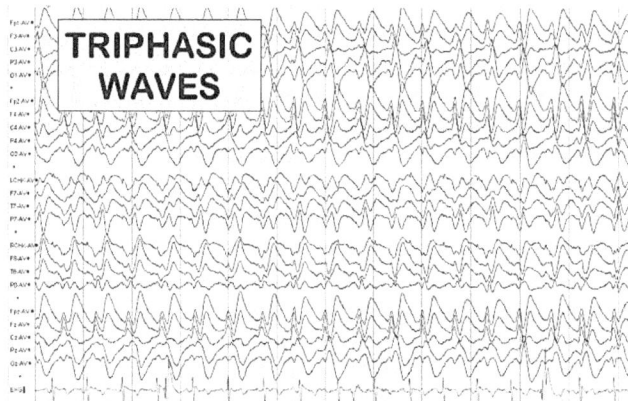

Triphasic waves, as shown in the above image, are indicative of what medical condition?
A. Meningitis
B. Cerebrovascular accident
C. Subacute sclerosis pan encephalitis
D. Hepatic encephalopathy

20.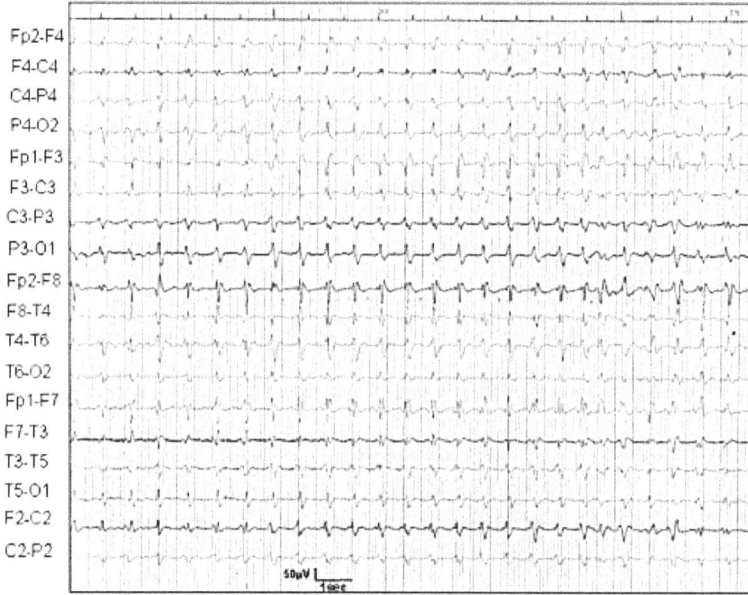

Which medical condition, shown in the above EEG, is characterized by the EEG showing slower than normal activity with loss of normal background and when the disease progresses shows burst of moderate voltage, biphasic and triphasic sharp waves in intervals of about 1 per second?
A. Meningitis
B. Creutzfeldt-Jakob Disease
C. Subacute sclerosis pan encephalitis
D. Hepatic encephalopathy

21. Which type of EEG activity most often appears in association with rapidly growing tumors such as glioblastoma and cerebral metastatic lesions?
    A. Polymorphic delta activity
    B. Triphasic waves
    C. Lower amplitude
    D. Sharp waves or spikes

22. Which is the MOST common EEG finding associated with Parkinson's disease?
    A. Non-specific slow wave activity
    B. Increased theta and delta activity
    C. Low voltage patterns of less than 10 microvolts and no organized rhythm
    D. No specific EEG findings are seen with Parkinson's disease

23. Low voltage, fast activity, lower amplitude, and decreased frequency alpha readings on an EKG are classic signs secondary to intake of which of the following?
    A. Alcohol
    B. Diazepam
    C. Phenobarbital
    D. Dilantin

24. _____ microamperes is the MAXIMUM leakage current permitted at the chassis when the ground wire is disabled.
    A. 100
    B. 200
    C. 300
    D. 400

25. Diffuse high amplitude beta activity on an EEG is common among individuals who have been administered which of the following?
    A. Alcohol
    B. Diazepam
    C. Phenobarbital
    D. Dilantin

KEY (CORRECT ANSWERS)

1.	A	11.	D
2.	B	12.	B
3.	C	13.	A
4.	D	14.	A
5.	D	15.	C
6.	A	16.	A
7.	A	17.	C
8.	A	18.	C
9.	D	19.	D
10.	D	20.	B

21. A
22. D
23. A
24. C
25. B

TEST 3

DIRECTIONS: Each question or incomplete statement is followed by several suggested answers or completions. Select the one that BEST answers the question or completes the statement. *PRINT THE LETTER OF THE CORRECT ANSWER IN THE SPACE AT THE RIGHT.*

1. Which of the following results when an atom has lost or gained one or more electrons?
   A. Ion   B. Positron   C. Proton   D. Prion

2. A(n) _____ is an elementary particle with a positive charge in the central nucleus of an atom.
   A. ion   B. positron   C. proton   D. electron

3. A(n) _____ is an elementary particle with a negative charge that orbits the nucleus of an atom.
   A. neutron   B. positron   C. proton   D. electron

4. When an atom is stable or in equilibrium, the number of protons is equal to the number of
   A. ions   B. positrons   C. protons   D. electrons

5. Which of the following is the property a circuit possesses that causes voltage to be induced in the circuit when there is a variation in current?
   A. Inductance   B. Impedance   C. Capacitance   D. Conductivity

6. Which of the following is the ability to store a charge?
   A. Inductance   B. Impedance   C. Capacitance   D. Conductivity

7. The inion is the most prominent projection of the _____ bone.
   A. occipital   B. zygomatic   C. sphenoid   D. ethmoid

8. _____ artifact is caused by movement of the tongue.
   A. Respiration   B. Glossokinetic
   C. Tremor   D. EKG

9. EKG artifact resembles _____ artifact on an EEG recording.
   A. muscle   B. electroretinogram
   C. IV   D. pulse

10. Which of the following is defined as a rhythmic activity elicited over the posterior head regions of the brain by repetitive photic stimulation at frequencies of 5-10 Hz?
    A. Hyperventilation   B. Photic driving
    C. Photoconvulsive response   D. Photomyoclonic response

11. According to ACNS guidelines, _____ minutes is the minimal amount of recording time acceptable when performing an EEG.
    A. 10 B. 20 C. 30 D. 40

12. According to ACNS guidelines, what are the appropriate filter settings when performing a clinical EEG?
    A. LFF < 1 and HFF > 70
    B. LFF > 1 and HFF < 70
    C. LFF > 0 and HFF < 100
    D. LFF < 0 and HFF > 100

13. According to ACNS guidelines, the inter-electrode impedance requirements when performing a clinical EEG are < _____ ohms.
    A. 1,000 B. 2,500 C. 5,000 D. 7,500

14. All of the following are valid reasons to have periods of eyes open/eyes closed during the performance of a clinical EEG EXCEPT:
    A. Some paroxysmal activity can only be seen with eye opening or eye closing
    B. Some rhythms can be masked by alpha activity with eyes closed
    C. To help differentiate cerebral activity from eye movement
    D. To help differentiate cerebral activity from glossokinetic artifact

15. According to ACNS guidelines, the inter-electrode distance requirement when performing an EEG to determine electrocerebral inactivity is > _____ cm.
    A. 2 B. 5 C. 10 D. 15

16. According to ACNS guidelines, the impedances should be _____ ohms and _____ ohms when recording electrocerebral inactivity.
    A. >100; <10,000
    B. >50; <5,000
    C. >50; <10,000
    D. >100; >10,000

17. Which of the following is a negative arch-shaped, 7-11 Hz rhythmic activity most often located in C3/C4?
    A. Alpha B. Beta C. Theta D. Mu

18. Which of the following is the beta frequency?
    A. 0-3 Hz B. 3-8 Hz C. 8-13 Hz D. >13 Hz

19. Which of the following is the delta frequency?
    A. 0-3 Hz B. 3-8 Hz C. 8-13 Hz D. >13 Hz

20. The _____ is alpha range activity located in the temporal region and commonly referred to as temporal-alpha rhythm.
    A. slow alpha variant
    B. third rhythm
    C. fast alpha variant
    D. rhythmic mid-temporal theta

21. Which of the following are positive 4-6 Hz theta waves in the occipital regions?
    A. Lambda B. Delta C. Theta D. Mu

22. Which of the following BEST describes positive occipital sharp transients (POSTS)?
    A. 0-3 Hz delta in the occipital region
    B. 4-6 Hz theta in the parietal region
    C. 4-6 Hz theta in the occipital region
    D. 8-10 Hz alpha in the parietal region

    22._____

23. _____ are sharply contoured waves located in the temporal region which can be seen bilaterally or independently and are characterized by no slow wave following the sharply contoured wave.
    A. Phantom spikes   B. Wicket spikes
    C. Pacemaker artifact   D. EKG artifact

    23._____

24. All of the following are types of cardiac artifacts associated with EEG recordings EXCEPT
    A. defibrillator   B. pacemaker
    C. pulse   D. ballistocardiographic

    24._____

25. What type of artifact results from head or body movements with cardiac contractions and is similar in morphology to pulse artifact but more widespread?
    A. defibrillator   B. pacemaker
    C. EKG   D. ballistocardiographic

    25._____

KEY (CORRECT ANSWERS)

1.	A	11.	B
2.	C	12.	A
3.	D	13.	C
4.	D	14.	D
5.	A	15.	C
6.	C	16.	A
7.	A	17.	D
8.	B	18.	D
9.	C	19.	A
10.	B	20.	B

21. A
22. C
23. B
24. A
25. D

TEST 4

DIRECTIONS: Each question or incomplete statement is followed by several suggested answers or completions. Select the one that BEST answers the question or completes the statement. *PRINT THE LETTER OF THE CORRECT ANSWER IN THE SPACE AT THE RIGHT.*

1. Which EEG artifact is characterized by low amplitude, typically only in one channel, and appears flat and close to isoelectric?
    A. Blink
    B. Eye flutter
    C. Salt bridge
    D. Lateral gaze

    1.____

2. Which EEG artifact is characterized by slow artifact seen in the frontal and temporal leads at a frequency of less than 1 Hz?
    A. Blink
    B. Eye flutter
    C. Salt bridge
    D. Lateral gaze

    2.____

3. Which EEG finding is MOST often associated with postnatal early infantile epileptic encephalopathy?
    A. Temporal sharp waves
    B. Hypsarrythmia
    C. Burst suppression
    D. Paroxysmal fast activity

    3.____

4. Which EEG finding is MOST often associated with infantile spasms?
    A. Temporal sharp waves
    B. Hypsarrythmia
    C. Burst suppression
    D. Paroxysmal fast activity

    4.____

5. Which EEG finding is MOST often associated with focal motor seizures?
    A. Temporal sharp waves
    B. Hypsarrythmia
    C. Burst suppression
    D. Frontocentral sharp activity

    5.____

6. Which EEG finding is MOST often associated with versive or sensory seizures?
    A. Temporal sharp waves
    B. Hypsarrythmia
    C. Burst suppression
    D. Frontocentral sharp activity

    6.____

7. The duration of a sharp wave is _____ milliseconds.
    A. 0-70   B. 70-200   C. 200-350   D. 350-500

    7.____

8. The duration of a spike is _____ milliseconds.
    A. 0-70   B. 70-200   C. 200-350   D. 350-500

    8.____

9. _____ is defined as the opposition to direct current flow and its unit of measure is the ohm.
    A. Resistance   B. Current   C. Impedance   D. Capacitance

    9.____

10. _____ is defined as the movement of electrons through a conductor and its unit of measure is the ampere.
    A. Resistance   B. Current   C. Impedance   D. Capacitance

    10.____

11. According to ACSN guidelines, the minimum sampling rate for EEG data should be at least _____ times the highest frequency setting.
    A. two
    B. three
    C. four
    D. five

12. Café-au-lait spots and neurofibromas are associated with which medical condition?
    A. Van Recklinghousen's disease
    B. Sturge-Weber syndrome
    C. Parkinson's disease
    D. Medullary blastoma

13. Port wine stain is associated with which medical condition?
    A. Van Recklinghousen's disease
    B. Sturge-Weber syndrome
    C. Parkinson's disease
    D. Medullary blastoma

14. Time constant is defined as the time required for the deflection to fall _____% of the peak deflection.
    A. 52
    B. 66
    C. 77
    D. 83

15. Even at therapeutic doses, antidepressants can cause a change of increased _____ activity to an EEG.
    A. alpha and theta
    B. theta and delta
    C. delta and beta
    D. theta and beta

16. The MINIMUM requirements for a monitor to display EEG are met with monitors that have at least _____ data points across the screen.
    A. 512
    B. 768
    C. 1,024
    D. 1,280

17. During the recording of cerebral activity, the calibration input voltage is changed from 50uV to 100uV. In what manner will the results be altered?
    A. Clipping of the waveform
    B. One-fold reduction of amplitude
    C. Two-fold increase in amplitude
    D. No effect on the activity being recorded

18. By what age should EEG differentiation of the four stages of non-REM sleep be identifiable in a child born at term?
    A. 1 week
    B. 1 month
    C. 6 months
    D. 1 year

19. Which of the following would produce an artifactual sharp wave recorded periodically by scalp leads and confirmed by the EKG monitoring channel?
    A. Eye movements
    B. Pulse
    C. Glossokinetic potentials
    D. Premature ventricular contractions

20. _____ is defined as a normal variant which occurs momentarily after eye closing and is a brief acceleration of the patient's normal alpha rhythm.
    A. Alpha squeak
    B. Slow alpha variant
    C. Paradoxical alpha response
    D. Temporal alpha response

21. _____ rhythm is a 6-11 Hz pattern associated with a skull defect.
    A. Mu
    B. Breach
    C. Midline theta
    D. Lambda

22. Short, heavy patients with broad necks produce the GREATEST amount of _____ artifact.
    A. respiration
    B. glossokinetic
    C. tremor
    D. EKG

23. A _____ montage is a montage that consists of an adjacent pair of electrodes of the 10-20 system of electrode placement.
    A. bipolar
    B. dipolar
    C. referential
    D. differential

24. _____ montage is similar to the common average reference, but instead refers one electrode to the nearest neighboring electrode, thus creating a local weighted average reference.
    A. Longitudinal bipolar
    B. Laplacian
    C. Transverse bipolar
    D. Weighted average

25. Which band of beta is primarily affected by drugs?
    A. 14-16 Hz
    B. 18-25 Hz
    C. 25-34 Hz
    D. 35-40 Hz

KEY (CORRECT ANSWERS)

1.	C	11.	B
2.	D	12.	A
3.	C	13.	B
4.	B	14.	C
5.	D	15.	D
6.	C	16.	C
7.	B	17.	D
8.	A	18.	C
9.	A	19.	D
10.	B	20.	A

21. B
22. D
23. A
24. B
25. B

EXAMINATION SECTION
TEST 1

DIRECTIONS: Each question or incomplete statement is followed by several suggested answers or completions. Select the one that BEST answers the question or completes the statement. *PRINT THE LETTER OF THE CORRECT ANSWER IN THE SPACE AT THE RIGHT.*

1. The particular combination of EEG electrodes used in recording brain activity, examined at a particular point in time, is referred to as the

    A. assemblage
    B. exemplar
    C. potential
    D. montage

2. For surgical situations, the BEST type of electrode to use is the

    A. spring-loaded
    B. collodion-attached
    C. needle type
    D. electrolyte paste-attached

3. The band of EEG frequencies that fall between 8/ and 13/sec are known as _____ waves.

    A. alpha   B. beta   C. theta   D. delta

4. Generally, the range of neurophysiological activity extends as high as _____ cycles/second.

    A. 750   B. 2000   C. 7000   D. 12,000

5. Nonepileptic attacks are essentially due to one of four causes. Which of the following is NOT one of these causes?

    A. Psychogenic alterations
    B. Sudden changes in blood chemistry
    C. Random neural firings
    D. Acute cerebral ischemia, caused by circulatory insufficiency

6. The brain receives its PRIMARY blood supply from the _____ arteries.

    A. basilar and jugular
    B. anterior and posterior communicating
    C. middle cerebral
    D. carotid and vertebral

7.

    Above is a surface recording made of EEG waves of the cerebral cortex.
    Which of the following laminar recordings would correspond to the above surface reading?

A. ～ᴧᴧ～ᴧ～ᴧᴧ～

B. ∿∿___∿∿

C. ～ᴧ～ᴧ～ᴧᴧ～

D. ∿∿⎴⎴

8. For EEG activity, it is generally accepted that a frequency displayed at _____ % or more of its actual voltage is acceptable.

   A. 60   B. 70   C. 80   D. 90

9. If an EEG is used to detect a possible asymmetry in the left temporal region, the left temporal electrodes should be referenced to the

   A. right free end of mandible
   B. right mastoid
   C. left ear
   D. right ear

10. What is the term for the vertical distance between two points in an EEG?

    A. Gain   B. Deflection
    C. Slope   D. Spike

11. Typically, an impedance of over _____ ohms in any electrode should not be accepted, and must be corrected before the machine begins to read.

    A. 750   B. 1000   C. 5000   D. 10,000

12. Another term for a montage in which electrodes are sequenced from the front of a subject's head to the back is

    A. AP   B. leeward   C. coronal   D. transverse

13. A patient in the acute stages of post-traumatic coma is displaying EEG abnormalities that are classified as Grade 4.
    The EEG will show

    A. predominant theta and little delta activity
    B. diffuse, mostly low-voltage delta and subdelta activity
    C. predominant delta and little theta activity
    D. isoelectric record

14. Of all brain tumors that are detected by EEG abnormalities, approximately what percentage can be localized in detail by use of the apparatus?

    A. 50   B. 70   C. 85   D. 100

15. Most EEG pens will provide good reproduction of activity up to _____ cycles/second.

    A. 100   B. 500   C. 3000   D. 7000

16. Artifacts that can be interpreted as brain activity are MOST commonly the result of

    A. failure to prepare skin surface
    B. parted but not completely severed wire leading from the electrode
    C. failure to check the impedance of electrodes
    D. the use of *flexible* collodion

17. The major class of artifacts perceived during EEG application is

    A. oculographic   B. cardiac
    C. sensorimotor   D. machine

18. *Beta* EEG frequencies fall into the range between _____ Hz.

    A. 0.1 to 3.5   B. 4 to 7.5
    C. 8 to 13   D. 14-40

19. Each of the following is an EEG abnormality that is associated with intracranial tumors EXCEPT

    A. spike and wave discharges
    B. focal slow-wave activity
    C. disturbance of the alpha rhythm
    D. diffuse or localized theta activity

20. Clinical labs in the United States typically use a paper speed of _____ mm/sec in EEG machines.

    A. 5   B. 15   C. 30   D. 50

21. Each of the following is among the nationally accepted technical standards required for the establishment of brain death by means of EEG recording EXCEPT

    A. recording to be made only by a neurophysician
    B. simultaneous ECG recording
    C. sensitivity increase up to 2 ?V/mm during most of the recording
    D. inter-electrode distances of at least 10 cm to enlarge the amplitudes

22. The part of the brain that controls motor movement is the posterior part of the _____ lobe.

    A. frontal   B. temporal   C. parietal   D. occipital

23. On most machines, it is BEST to try to arrive at calibration signals with deflections somewhere between

    A. 0.5-1.0 mm   B. 1-3 mm
    C. 5-12 mm   D. 1-3 cm

24. Most modern-day EEG machines have a noise level of _____ µV/mm.

   A. 0.5 B. 1 C. 2 D. 4

25. Which of the following conditions is MOST likely indicated by the simple EEG recording shown below?

   EEG ─────────────

   A. Stage 3 sleep
   B. Hypercapnia
   C. Arousal
   D. Grade 4 post-traumatic coma

KEY (CORRECT ANSWERS)

1. D		11. C	
2. B		12. A	
3. A		13. B	
4. B		14. B	
5. C		15. A	
6. D		16. C	
7. C		17. D	
8. B		18. D	
9. D		19. B	
10. B		20. C	

21. A
22. A
23. C
24. C
25. B

TEST 2

DIRECTIONS: Each question or incomplete statement is followed by several suggested answers or completions. Select the one that BEST answers the question or completes the statement. *PRINT THE LETTER OF THE CORRECT ANSWER IN THE SPACE AT THE RIGHT.*

Questions 1-4.

DIRECTIONS: Questions 1 through 4 refer to the diagram below, a template for electrode placement on a patient's head. Assume that all electrode placements refer to the international 10-20 system of placement.

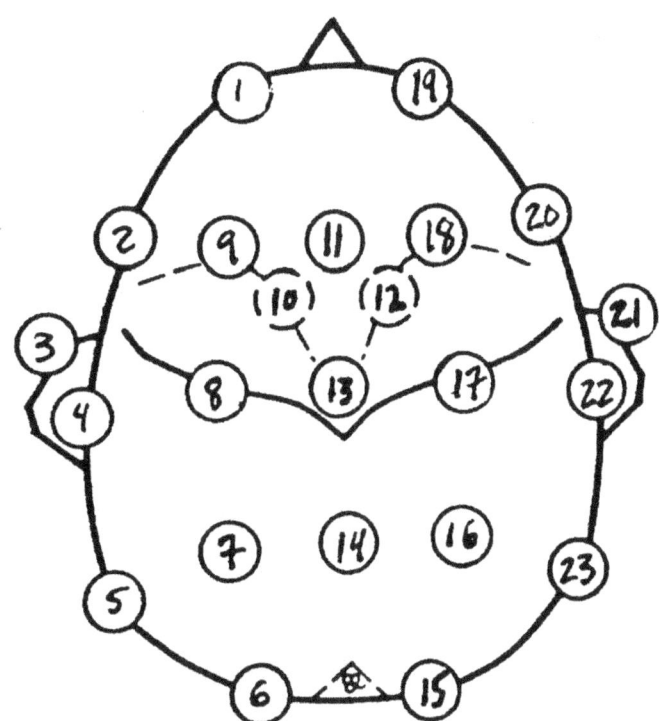

1. Which electrode is indicated by #11? 1.____
   A. O_1 B. F_z C. C_z D. F_p1

2. Which electrode is indicated by #5? 2.____
   A. T_5 B. F_4 C. P_z D. A_1

3. Which electrode is indicated by #21? 3.____
   A. T_3 B. A_2 C. P_z D. F_p2

4. Which electrode is indicated by #15? 4.____
   A. T_6 B. O_2 C. P_4 D. F_z

5. A technician compares a subject's simultaneous EEG and ECG readouts. MOST likely, the technician is 5.____

A. checking the cardiac-brainstem neural link activity
B. looking for evidence of cerebrovascular problems
C. looking for asymmetrical activity
D. checking the EEG for artifacts

6. Calibration signals are NOT used to

   A. provide a display of possible artifacts indicating impedance failure
   B. provide a display of the sharpness of the square wave for some suggestion of the effect of high-frequency filters
   C. assess pen alignment and time axis
   D. provide a sample of the rise time

7. Which of the following EEG findings is MOST likely to be associated with acute encephalitis?

   A. Unilateral epileptiform abnormalities
   B. Intermittent rhythmic delta activity
   C. Focal slow-wave abnormalities
   D. Mild to severe slow-wave abnormalities

8. If two electrodes are demonstrating the same 100-μV delta wave and there is no activity in either electrode that is different from the other, connection of the two electrodes to an amplifier will result in a(n)

   A. flat line
   B. spike
   C. attenuation
   D. machine artifact

9. When the membrane of a nerve cell body is penetrated by a microelectrode, a potential of about _____ mV with negative polarity in the intracellular space can be recorded.

   A. 30-40
   B. 60-70
   C. 85-100
   D. 120-160

10. For patients aged 21-40, the MOST common cause of epileptic attacks is

    A. CNS infection
    B. chronic alcoholism
    C. benign rolandic epilepsy
    D. trauma

11. A patient in the acute stages of post-traumatic coma is displaying EEG abnormalities that are classified as Grade 2.
    The EEG will show

    A. predominant theta and little delta activity
    B. generalized epileptiform abnormalities
    C. diffuse, mostly low-voltage delta and subdelta activity
    D. intermittent rhythmic delta activity

12. Which of the following is NOT a problem associated with the use of electrolyte paste for the attachment of electrodes?

    A. Overdrying
    B. Patient discomfort due to physical perception of current flow
    C. Shorting out between electrodes caused by too-liberal application
    D. Variable contact

13. If an oculographic artifact interferes with an EEG display, the BEST remedy is to place an electrode _____ , and to reference the front polar electrode to the subject's ear.

    A. directly above the sinus
    B. at the mastoid
    C. beneath the center of the eye
    D. at the sternoclavicular joint

14. Typically, the upper frequency of spike discharges is about _____ cycles/second.

    A. 15   B. 50   C. 85   D. 105

15. More than 50% of cerebral arterial thrombosis is preceded by a condition known as

    A. transient ischemic attack
    B. cerebral infarction
    C. subclavian steal
    D. intracerebral steal

16. Which of the following would MOST likely be an indicator of rising electrode impedance?

    A. The pen going off-line for a brief period, and then correcting itself
    B. A 60-cycle artifact
    C. Poor calibration
    D. Lengths of flat line

17. The trigeminal nerve attaches itself at the

    A. midbrain   B. medulla   C. pons   D. cerebrum

18. The band of EEG frequencies under 3.5/sec are known as _____ waves.

    A. alpha   B. beta   C. theta   D. delta

19. If long-term contact of an electrode is expected, the electrolyte compound used must NOT contain

    A. magnesium   B. carbon   C. calcium   D. potassium

20. The classical EEG correlate for a state of relaxed wakefulness is the _____ rhythm.

    A. rolandic   B. alpha   C. beta   D. central

21. Which of the following conditions is MOST likely indicated, by the simple EEG recording shown below?

    EEG ―――――――

    A. Syncope   B. Stage 4 sleep
    C. Voluntary eye scanning   D. Asphyxia

22. An anterior temporal rhythm in the alpha range in an EEG is referred to as a(n) _____ rhythm.

    A. lambda   B. breach   C. kappa   D. central

23. If an EEG display shows a loss of low-voltage signals, which of the following is the MOST likely cause? 23.___

    A. Electrodes becoming intermittently unfixed
    B. Flattening of pen motor ball bearings
    C. Absence-type epileptic attack
    D. Improper lowering of skin impedance

24. A 60-cycle artifact appears in an EEG. 24.___
    Which of the following is MOST likely to have caused it?

    A. The ground loop   B. Motor activity
    C. Sudden subject arousal   D. Cardiac activity

25. Which of the following steps in applying a collodion-fixed electrode would be performed FIRST? 25.___

    A. Compressed air is sprayed to dry the glue against the skin.
    B. A piece of gauze soaked in collodion is placed over the electrode.
    C. A blunt-tipped needle is used to add electrolyte solution into the hole in the electrode.
    D. The electrode is placed in position on the head.

KEY (CORRECT ANSWERS)

1.	B	11.	A
2.	A	12.	B
3.	B	13.	C
4.	B	14.	B
5.	D	15.	A
6.	A	16.	B
7.	D	17.	C
8.	A	18.	D
9.	B	19.	C
10.	D	20.	B

21. D
22. C
23. B
24. A
25. D

EXAMINATION SECTION
TEST 1

DIRECTIONS: Each question or incomplete statement is followed by several suggested answers or completions. Select the one that BEST answers the question or completes the statement. *PRINT THE LETTER OF THE CORRECT ANSWER IN THE SPACE AT THE RIGHT.*

1. An EEG shows suppression of activity over an entire hemisphere. MOST likely, the patient is experiencing

    A. a fungal disease   B. epilepsy syndrome
    C. meningitis   D. viral disease

2. The voltage of an EEG signal can be determined to be the product of

    A. sensitivity and amplitude
    B. pen deflection and gain
    C. amplitude and gain
    D. pen deflection and sensitivity

3. The part of the brain that is concerned with vision is the _____ lobe.

    A. frontal   B. temporal   C. parietal   D. occipital

4. Electrocerebral silence can only be taken as a sign of brain death under certain circumstances.
   Which of the following is NOT one of these circumstances?

    A. Neurologic signs of cortical and brainstem functions are lacking
    B. The existence of marked hypothermia
    C. ECS lasts for a distinct length of time
    D. Intoxication is excluded from consideration

5. A low-voltage record is defined as one characterized by activity of amplitudes not greater than _____ microvolts over all head regions.

    A. 2   B. 5   C. 20   D. 40

6. A high-frequency filter will affect a designated frequency by about _____ %.

    A. 5-10   B. 10-20   C. 20-30   D. 30-40

7. What is the term for the ratio of output signal voltage to input signal voltage in an EEG channel?

    A. Resistance   B. Gain
    C. Sensitivity   D. Amplitude

8. *Rolandic mu* or central EEG rhythms are MOST frequently blocked by

    A. viral disease   B. pupil dilation
    C. fungal disease   D. movement

9. On a properly measured head, an electrode placement that deviates more than _____ from the template specification should be corrected as soon as it is discovered.

   A. 2 mm   B. B, 0.5 cm   C. 1 cm   D. 3 cm

10. Each of the following nerves attaches at the junction of the pons and the medulla EXCEPT the _____ nerve.

    A. facial
    B. oculomotor
    C. auditory
    D. abducens

11. According to the American EEG Society's standards, 8- or 10-channel recordings require the use of AT LEAST montages from the standardized list.

    A. 3   B. 5   C. 7   D. 9

12. The brain's cerebrospinal fluid is produced by a body known as the

    A. aqueduct of Sylvius
    B. lateral geniculate body
    C. angular gyrus
    D. choroid plexus

13. The size of a glial cell's membrane potential approximates the _____ potential of nerve cells.

    A. inhibitory synaptic
    B. potassium equilibrium
    C. sodium threshold
    D. membrane

14. A patient in the acute stages of post-traumatic coma is displaying EEG abnormalities that are classified as Grade 1.
    The EEG will show

    A. predominant alpha and little theta activity
    B. polymorphic delta activity
    C. isoelectric record
    D. paroxysmal slow waves

15. A technician constructs a reference montage with electrodes from one hemisphere in sequence. MOST likely, the EEG is being used to detect

    A. a tumor or lesion
    B. possible brain death
    C. an area of focal delta activity
    D. the effect of craniocerebral trauma

16. The MOST frequently perceived artifacts in all EEG applications are related to

    A. the ground loop
    B. cardiac activity
    C. nearby equipment
    D. electrodes

17. What part of the brain is MOST responsible for determining human behavior?

    A. Hippocampus
    B. Frontal lobe
    C. Limbic lobe
    D. Pons

18. Unless there is a clear indication to contrary, an EEG montage should PROBABLY be changed every

    A. 30 seconds
    B. 2-3 minutes
    C. 5-10 minutes
    D. 15-30 minutes

19. Which of the following EEG findings is MOST likely to be associated with multiple sclerosis?

    A. Hypsarrhythmia
    B. Generalized delta slowing
    C. Periodic lateralized epileptiform discharges
    D. Focal slow-wave abnormalities

20. Generally, as inter-electrode distance *increases,*

    A. higher voltages are seen
    B. waveforms increase in complexity
    C. greater skin impedance is required
    D. lower alpha activity is seen

21. A patient is in the late diencephalic stage of post-traumatic coma. Which of the following symptoms will be displayed?

    A. Eyes immobile, straight ahead
    B. Decerebrate response to pain stimulus
    C. Eyes roving
    D. Flaccid limbs

22. Which of the following is NOT among the nationally accepted technical standards required for the establishment of brain death by means of EEG recordings?

    A. Use of time constants of 0.3 to 0.4 seconds
    B. Recording time of at least 30 minutes
    C. Inter-electrode impedances under 10,000ft but over 100ft
    D. A minimum of five scalp electrodes

23. *Alpha dropout* in an EEG characterizes the earliest stage of

    A. cerebrovascular accident
    B. dementia
    C. drowsiness
    D. epileptiform activity

24. Most modern-day EEG machines allow recordings with a sensitivity of _____ V/mm.

    A. 0.3 to 0.4
    B. 0.5 to 1
    C. 0.75 to 1.5
    D. 1 to 2

25. The MOST frequently occurring, and most troublesome, cardiac artifact to interfere with EEG readouts is the _____ artifact.

    A. ECG
    B. ballistocardiographic
    C. motor
    D. pulsation

KEY (CORRECT ANSWERS)

1.	B	11.	C
2.	D	12.	D
3.	D	13.	B
4.	B	14.	A
5.	C	15.	C
6.	C	16.	D
7.	B	17.	C
8.	D	18.	B
9.	C	19.	D
10.	B	20.	A

21. A
22. D
23. C
24. B
25. A

TEST 2

DIRECTIONS: Each question or incomplete statement is followed by several suggested answers or completions. Select the one that BEST answers the question or completes the statement. *PRINT THE LETTER OF THE CORRECT ANSWER IN THE SPACE AT THE RIGHT.*

Questions 1-10.

DIRECTIONS: Questions 1 through 10 refer to the figure below, a diagram of several regions of the brain. Place the letter that corresponds to each region in the space at the right of the region's name. Assume that the subject is right-handed.

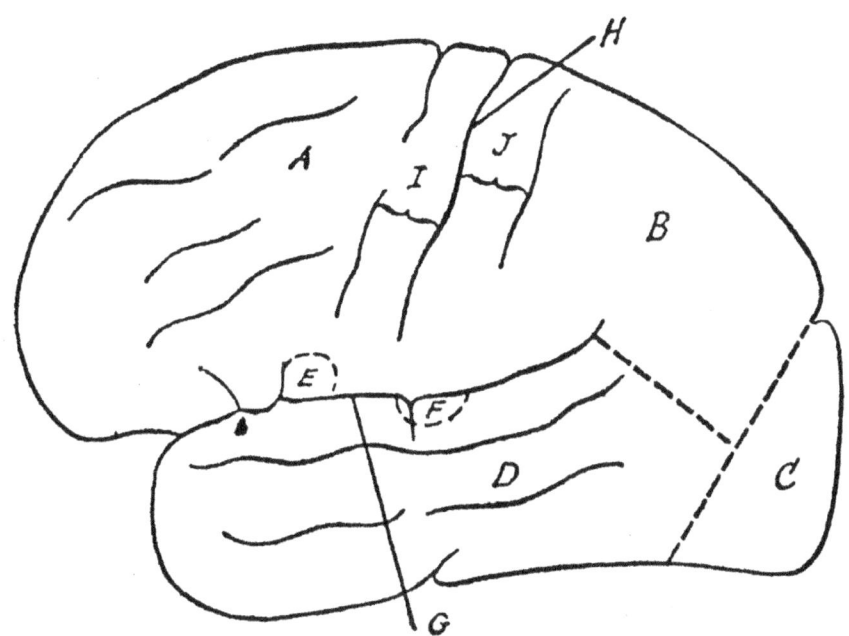

1. Lateral sulcus   1.____
2. Temporal lobe   2.____
3. Central sulcus   3.____
4. Precentral gyrus   4.____
5. Occipital lobe   5.____
6. Motor-speech area   6.____
7. Frontal lobe   7.____
8. Auditory cortex   8.____
9. Postcentral gyrus   9.____
10. Parietal lobe   10.____

11. Each of the following is a situation in which a technician might use a slower paper speed with an EEG machine EXCEPT

    A. to check for ECG artifacts in the EEG display
    B. monitoring repetitive episodes of high voltage spike
    C. detecting subtle asymmetries of slow activity
    D. sleep studies

12. Voluntary scanning eye movements play a MOST significant role in precipitating _____ waves in an EEG.

    A. breach   B. lambda   C. central   D. theta

13. In general, the HIGHEST voltages recorded from a normal adult subject will occur within the frequencies of _____ waves.

    A. alpha   B. beta   C. theta   D. delta

14. If a patient experiences a midbrain hemorrhage, the EEG will MOST likely show

    A. focal activity in the alpha range
    B. high-voltage slow waves
    C. diffuse activity in the upper theta range
    D. total hemispheric silence

15. Which of the following conditions is MOST likely indicated by the simple EEG recording shown below?

    A. Arousal   B. Seizure
    C. Stage 1 sleep   D. Relaxed wakefulness

16. What type of EEG frequencies seem to play an important role ONLY during infancy and childhood?

    A. Theta   B. Alpha
    C. Rolandic mu   D. Kappa

17. The brain's auditory cortex is located on the superior internal portion of the _____ lobe.

    A. frontal   B. temporal   C. parietal   D. occipital

18. Which of the following methods for EEG analysis is classified as *nonparametric*?

    A. Amplitude distributions   B. Mimetic analysis
    C. Segmentation analysis   D. Time-varying spectra

19. *Theta* EEG frequencies fall into the range between _____ Hz.

    A. 0.1 to 3.5   B. 4 to 7.5
    C. 8 to 13   D. 14-40

20. The frontal lobe of the brain is divided from the parietal lobe by the   20._____

    A. angular gyrus B. central sulcus
    C. arachnoid   D. lateral sulcus

21. The effect of a low frequency filter used with an EEG is directly dependent on   21._____

    A. the time constant involved
    B. the type of amplifier used
    C. the nature of brain activity being measured
    D. electrode impedance

22. Spikes in the tonic phase of generalized seizure occur within the approximate range of _____ cycles/second.   22._____

    A. 5-12   B. 13-20   C. 21-27   D. 25-32

23. MOST incidents of stroke are caused by   23._____

    A. cerebral hemorrhage
    B. subdural hematoma
    C. thrombosis of a cerebral artery
    D. embolism

24. In most applications, the *slow* paper speed for an EEG machine is _____ mm/sec.   24._____

    A. 5   B. 15   C. 30   D. 50

25. An EEG shows diffuse slow-wave abnormalities. MOST likely, the patient is experiencing   25._____

    A. slow virus disease   B. encephalitis
    C. C. fungal disease   D. a glioma

KEY (CORRECT ANSWERS)

1. G		11. A
2. D		12. B
3. H		13. D
4. I		14. C
5. C		15. B
6. E		16. A
7. A		17. B
8. F		18. A
9. J		19. B
10. B		20. B

21. A
22. B
23. C
24. B
25. C

EXAMINATION SECTION
TEST 1

DIRECTIONS: Each question or incomplete statement is followed by several suggested answers or completions. Select the one that BEST answers the question or completes the statement. *PRINT THE LETTER OF THE CORRECT ANSWER IN THE SPACE AT THE RIGHT.*

Questions 1-6.

DIRECTIONS: Questions 1 through 6 refer to the figure below, a diagram of the meningal layers of the brain. Place the letter that corresponds to each part in the space at the right next to its name.

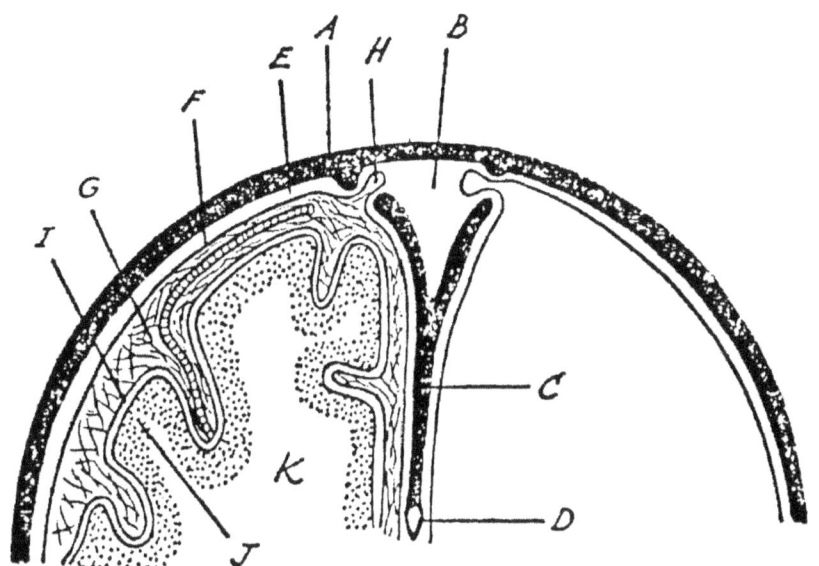

1. Arachnoid   1.____

2. Inferior sagittal sinus   2.____

3. Pia mater   3.____

4. Superior sagittal sinus   4.____

5. Dura mater   5.____

6. Falx cerebri   6.____

7. In order to avoid using an earlobe electrode with an epileptic subject, reference electrodes should be placed at the   7.____

    A. sternoclavicular joint and the first thoracic vertebra
    B. mastoids
    C. nasal bridge and the lower occipital
    D. free ends of the mandible

8. A patient in the acute stages of post-traumatic coma is displaying EEG abnormalities that are classified as Grade 5.
   The EEG will show

   A. slowing of the background
   B. predominant alpha and little theta activity
   C. isoelectric record
   D. focal slow-wave abnormalities

9. Which of the following is NOT a pre-EEG activation procedure used for patients with latent cerebrovascular disorders?

   A. Hyperventilation
   B. Aortic massage
   C. Neck rotation
   D. Carotid compression

10. If a ballistocardiographic artifact interferes with an EEG display, the BEST remedy is to

    A. move the appropriate electrode
    B. re-establish the ground loop
    C. place a pillow under the subject's neck
    D. change the subject's level of consciousness

11. Which of the following is NOT an EEG abnormality that is associated with intracranial tumors?

    A. Localized loss of activity over the area of the tumor
    B. Generalized delta slowing
    C. Monorhythmic sinusoidal delta activity
    D. Polymorphic delta activity

12. The optic nerve attaches at the

    A. midbrain   B. medulla   C. pons   D. cerebrum

13. On nost machines with narrow pen spacing, the calibration signal deflections cannot exceed _____ without exceeding the accurate arch of each pen.

    A. 1mm   B. 5 mm   C. 10 mm   D. 3 cm

14. What is the term for the ratio of input voltage to output pen deflection in an EEG channel?

    A. Sensitivity
    B. Amplitude
    C. Gain
    D. Differential

15. The _____ of the brain is especially important in highest mental functions and the determination of personality.

    A. hippocampus
    B. pons
    C. prefrontal cortex
    D. medulla

16. Typically, a 35 cycles/second filter will reduce activity of 50 cycles/second to about _____ % of its true amplitude.

    A. 50   B. 60   C. 70   D. 80

17. Rhythmic beta activity is found CHIEFLY over the _____ region of the brain.   17.____
    A. anterior and central   B. frontal and central
    C. superior   D. anterior

18. Which of the following is a situation in which a technician might choose to use a faster   18.____
    paper speed for an EEG machine?
    A. Studies of premature infants
    B. Defining wave amplitudes
    C. Studies of asymmetrical onset of seemingly synchronous activity
    D. Detecting sudden drops in voltage

19. Another term for a montage in which electrodes are sequenced from one side of a subject's head to the other is   19.____
    A. AP   B. temporal
    C. coronal   D. longitudinal

20. The American EEG Society defines *electrocerebral activity* as no activity above _____ microvolts.   20.____
    A. 0.5   B. 2   C. 4   D. 6

21. In general, the LOWEST voltages recorded from a normal adult subject will occur within the frequencies of _____ waves.   21.____
    A. alpha   B. beta   C. theta   D. delta

22. A visual reader of an EEG typically has the ability to see changes that involve deflections of _____ mm and higher.   22.____
    A. 10   B. 5   C. 1   D. 0.5

23. Which of the following is NOT a typical EEG event in a vasodepressive syncopal attack?   23.____
    A. Alpha depression
    B. Low-voltage fast activity
    C. Theta activity of decreasing voltage
    D. High-voltage delta activity

24. The American EEG Society recommends that activity of 70 cycles/second should NOT be attenuated by more than _____ dB.   24.____
    A. .05   B. 1   C. 3   D. 4.5

25. A technician uses low linear frequency to change the apparent peak of an observed slow wave.   25.____
    This effect is called
    A. sublimation   B. phase shifting
    C. slow spiking   D. low-pass filtering

KEY (CORRECT ANSWERS)

1.	F	11.	B
2.	D	12.	D
3.	I	13.	C
4.	B	14.	A
5.	A	15.	C
6.	C	16.	B
7.	A	17.	B
8.	C	18.	C
9.	B	19.	C
10.	C	20.	B

21. B
22. D
23. C
24. C
25. B

TEST 2

DIRECTIONS: Each question or incomplete statement is followed by several suggested answers or completions. Select the one that BEST answers the question or completes the statement. *PRINT THE LETTER OF THE CORRECT ANSWER IN THE SPACE AT THE RIGHT.*

Questions 1-8.

DIRECTIONS: Questions 1 through 8 refer to the figure below, a diagram of the major arteries supplying blood to the brain. Place the letter that corresponds to each artery or set of arteries in the space at the right, next to the appropriate name.

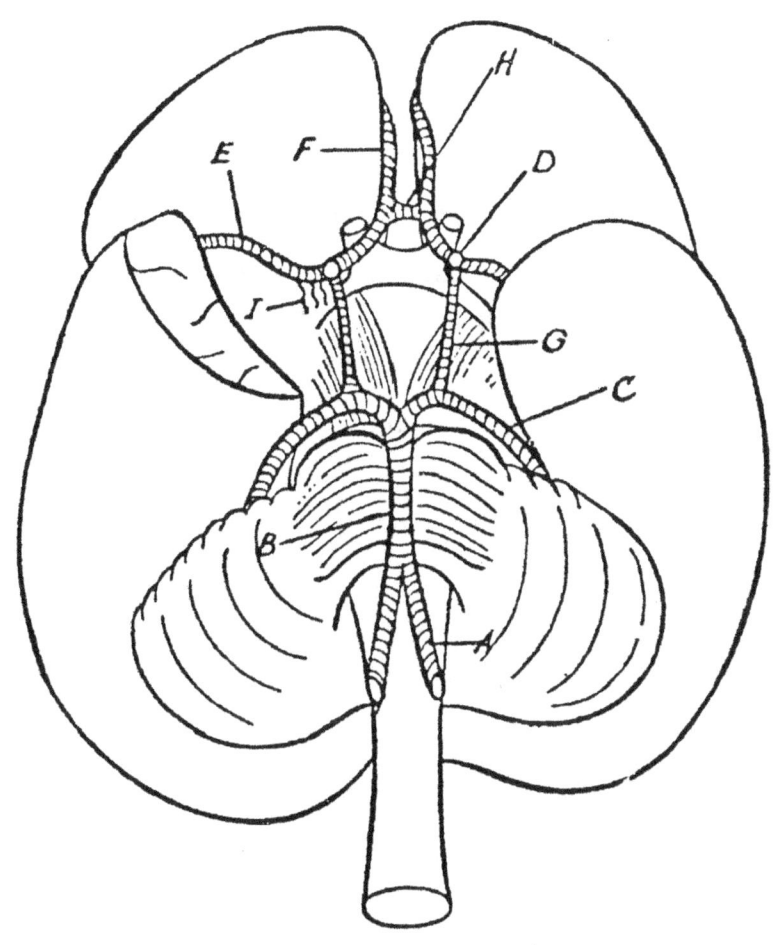

1. Anterior communicating artery   1.____
2. Posterior cerebral arteries   2.____
3. Vertebral arteries   3.____
4. Internal carotid   4.____
5. Middle cerebral artery   5.____
6. Basilar artery   6.____

7. Posterior communicating artery 7.___

8. Anterior cerebral artery 8.___

9. For patients aged 4 months to 2 years, the MOST common cause of epileptic attacks is 9.___

    A. trauma
    B. febrile convulsions
    C. residual epilepsy due to early CNS damage
    D. arterial occlusion

10. A patient in the acute stages of post-traumatic coma is displaying EEG abnormalities that are classified as Grade 3. 10.___
    The EEG will show

    A. predominant theta and little delta activity
    B. predominant high-voltage rhythmic and arrhythmic delta and subdelta activity
    C. intermittent slow-wave bursts
    D. diffuse, mostly low-voltage delta and subdelta activity

11. Generally, the amplitudes of scalp EEG lie between _____ microvolts in normal adult subjects. 11.___

    A. 5-12   B. 10-50   C. 20-70   D. 50-100

12. According to the American EEG Society's standards, when 16-channel or larger machines are used, _____ montages will be needed. 12.___

    A. at least 1 from each of the 3 classes
    B. 5
    C. at least 2 from each of the 3 classes
    D. 7

13. A patient is in the midbrain upper-pons stage of post-traumatic coma. 13.___
    Which of the following symptoms will be displayed?

    A. Nonstereotyped movement of the arms and legs
    B. Roving eye movements
    C. Enlarged pupils
    D. Ataxia

14. Which of the following nerves does NOT attach to the medulla? 14.___

    A. Hypoglossal   B. Accessory
    C. Trochlear   D. Vagus

15. Which region of the brain receives the HIGHEST levels of cerebral blood flow? 15.___

    A. Medulla   B. Anterior
    C. Superior   D. Frontal-central

16. If two electrodes are connected to an EEG amplifier and the result is a flat line, it is an indication that the 16.___

    A. activity is of equal potential in both electrodes
    B. amplifier is not functioning

C. tested portion of the brain is inactive
D. subject is in a stage IV coma

17. The olfactory bulb and nerves are located beneath the _____ lobe of the brain.

    A. frontal   B. temporal   C. parietal   D. occipital

18. What is the term for the voltage of an EEG wave measured peak to peak?

    A. Amplitude   B. Frequency   C. Gain   D. Impedance

19. The hypothalamus is connected to the medial part of the _____ lobe of the brain.

    A. frontal   B. temporal   C. parietal   D. occipital

20. Each of the following is a common disadvantage associated with the use of bipolar montages EXCEPT

    A. creation of out-of-phase relations that are hard to distinguish from true psychological out-of-phase voltages
    B. occasional reduction of voltages to vanishing point
    C. overall increase in the number of machine artifacts
    D. creation of complex waveforms

21. Which of the following EEG findings is MOST likely to be associated with Creutzfeldt-Jakob disease?

    A. Generalized periodic sharp waves
    B. Intermittent slow-wave bursts
    C. Focal slow-wave abnormalities
    D. Focal delta slowing

22. Posterior alpha rhythms are MOST frequently blocked by

    A. psychosis   B. motor activity
    C. coughing   D. eye opening

23. Collodion-attached electrodes can be left in place for up to _____ if long-term contact is expected, without any perceivable skin effects.

    A. 18 hours   B. 48 hours
    C. 5 days   D. 10 days

24. When using a low-frequency filter with an EEG apparatus, a time constant of _____ would be appropriate in almost all records.

    A. .03-.04   B. .05-.01   C. 0.3-0.4   D. 0.7-1

25. If a pulsation artifact is interfering with an EEG readout, the BEST solution is to

    A. move the appropriate electrode
    B. re-establish the ground loop
    C. move the subject's head
    D. change the subject's level of consciousness

4 (#2)

KEY (CORRECT ANSWERS)

1. H
2. C
3. A
4. D
5. E

6. B
7. G
8. F
9. B
10. B

11. B
12. A
13. C
14. C
15. D

16. A
17. A
18. A
19. B
20. C

21. A
22. D
23. C
24. C
25. A

EXAMINATION SECTION
TEST 1

DIRECTIONS: Each question or incomplete statement is followed by several suggested answers or completions. Select the one that BEST answers the question or completes the statement. *PRINT THE LETTER OF THE CORRECT ANSWER IN THE SPACE AT THE RIGHT.*

1. Slower chart speed is useful in EEG applications as an aid in identifying _____ -wave activity.

   A. alpha B. beta C. delta D. theta

2. The input voltage (μv) on grid 1 of an EEG's differential amplifier is -20; and the input voltage for grid 2 is -30. The output voltage will be _____ μv.

   A. -10 B. 10 C. -50 D. 50

3. For EEG applications, a machine that displays AT LEAST _____ derivations is necessary.

   A. 4 B. 8 C. 16 D. 21

4. What is the term for the electrode landmark that is located at the indentation where the nose joins the forehead?

   A. Nasion B. Pre-auricular point
   C. Inion   D. Septum

5. If a single EEG channel appears to be completely dead, the MOST likely source of the trouble is the

   A. amplifier   B. input board
   C. chart drive D. pen motor

6. The control element in an amplifier vacuum tube is the

   A. base B. grid C. chart D. fuse

7. Which of the following electrodes is known as the vertex electrode?

   A. O1 B. Cz C. Fpz D. Pz

8. A technician uses an ordinary ohmmeter to check the grounding of an EEG machine. If one probe is connected to the chassis and another to a cold-water pipe in the room, the machine will be safely grounded if the pointer of the meter is deflected to the right and reads _____ Ω or less.

   A. 2 B. 10 C. 20 D. 35

9.

[EEG tracing with channels F7-Fp1, Fp1-Fp2, Fp2-F8, F7-F3, F3-Fz, Fz-F4, F4-F8, T3-C3, C3-Cz, Cz-C4, C4-T4, T5-P3, P3-Pz, Pz-P4, P4-T6, T5-O1, O1-O2, O2-T6]

In the figure above, a diagram of an 18-channel EEG, what is indicated by the bold arrows?
A(n)

- A. K complex
- B. eye-open artifact
- C. muscle artifact
- D. 60-cycle artifact

10. When grid 2 of one EEG channel and grid 1 of another channel are both connected to a single electrode situated over a focus of activity, _____ occurs.

- A. inversion
- B. instrumental phase reversal
- C. cancellation
- D. summation

11. What is the term for inherent currents that flow between the AC power line and the chassis of the EEG machine?

- A. Leakage current
- B. Master channel
- C. Voltage current
- D. Phase-in

12. What is the generalized term for any isolated EEG wave that stands out from the background activity?

- A. Spike
- B. Complex
- C. Transient
- D. Polarity

13. In establishing the positions of coronal ear-to-ear electrodes, which of the following steps would be performed FIRST? 13.____

    A. Mark midline central position
    B. Mark location of right temporal region
    C. Mark
    D. Compute 10% and 20% of distance from ear point to ear point

Question 14.

DIRECTIONS: Question 14 refers to the information below: four representations of EEG montages labeled 1, 2, 3, and 4. Study each montage and then answer Question 14.

Channel No.	Montage #1	Montage #2	Montage #3	Montage #4
1	Fpl-F7	F7-Fpl	F7-A1	Fpl-F3
2	F7-T3	Fpl-Fp2	F8-A2	F3-C3
3	T3-T5	Fp2-F8	T3-A1	C3-P3
4	T5-01	T3-C3	T4-A2	P3-01
5	Fp2-F8	C3-Cz	T5-A1	Fp2-F4
6	F8-T4	Cz-C4	T6-A2	F4-C4
7	T4-T6	C4-T4	Fpl-Al	C4-P4
8	T6-02	T5-01	Fp2-A2	P4-02
9	Fpl-F3	01-02	F3-A1	Fz-Cz
10	F3-C3	02-T6	F4-A2	Cz-Pz
11	C3-P3		C3-A1	
12	P3-01		C4-A2	
13	Fp2-F4		P3-A1	
14	F4-C4		P4-A2	
15	C4-P4		01-A2	
16	P4-O2		02-A2	
17	Fz-Cz		Fz-Al	
18	Cz-Pz		Pz-A2	

14. Which of the montages above is a transverse bipolar montage? 14.____

    A. 1   B. 2   C. 3   D. 4

15. The LAST component of a technician's EEG report is generally 15.____

    A. descriptive details regarding the testing situation
    B. correlation of EEG findings with the clinical profile
    C. a brief history and the clinical findings to date
    D. description of the EEG and the state of the patient

16. When photic stimulation is used for EEG purposes, the stimulus should be placed approximately _____ cm in front of the subject's eyes. 16.____

    A. 10   B. 30   C. 90   D. 150

17. What should a technician do FIRST in order to identify or rule out the external environment as a source of EEG artifacts? 17.____

    A. Short-circuit the inputs of all channels
    B. Check the master channel

C. Clean all switch contacts
D. Switch to calibration

18. If used as an activation procedure, and unless contra-indicated, hyperventilation should be performed by a subject for a duration of AT LEAST

    A. 30 seconds
    B. 60 seconds
    C. 3 minutes
    D. 7 minutes

19. In establishing the locations of all 19 scalp electrodes, which of the following electrodes is generally marked LAST?

    A. F3
    B. P3
    C. Cz
    D. 01

20. According to the American EEG Society's recommendations, a recording electrode should NOT significantly attenuate signals between _____ Hz.

    A. 0.5-40
    B. 0.5-70
    C. 5-75
    D. 25-220

21. The MOST important use of a marker channel with EEG machines is to

    A. supply coded deflection patterns
    B. detect single-channel artifacts
    C. identify chart speed
    D. reference patient reactions to intentional photic stimuli

22. Which type of electrode is used specifically for recording activity from the uncus and hippocampus?

    A. Subdural
    B. Clip
    C. Nasopharyngeal
    D. Epidural

Questions 23-25.

DIRECTIONS: Questions 23 through 25 refer to the figure shown on the following page, a diagram of an 18-channel EEG recorded during sleep. Study the EEG and then answer Questions 23 through 25.

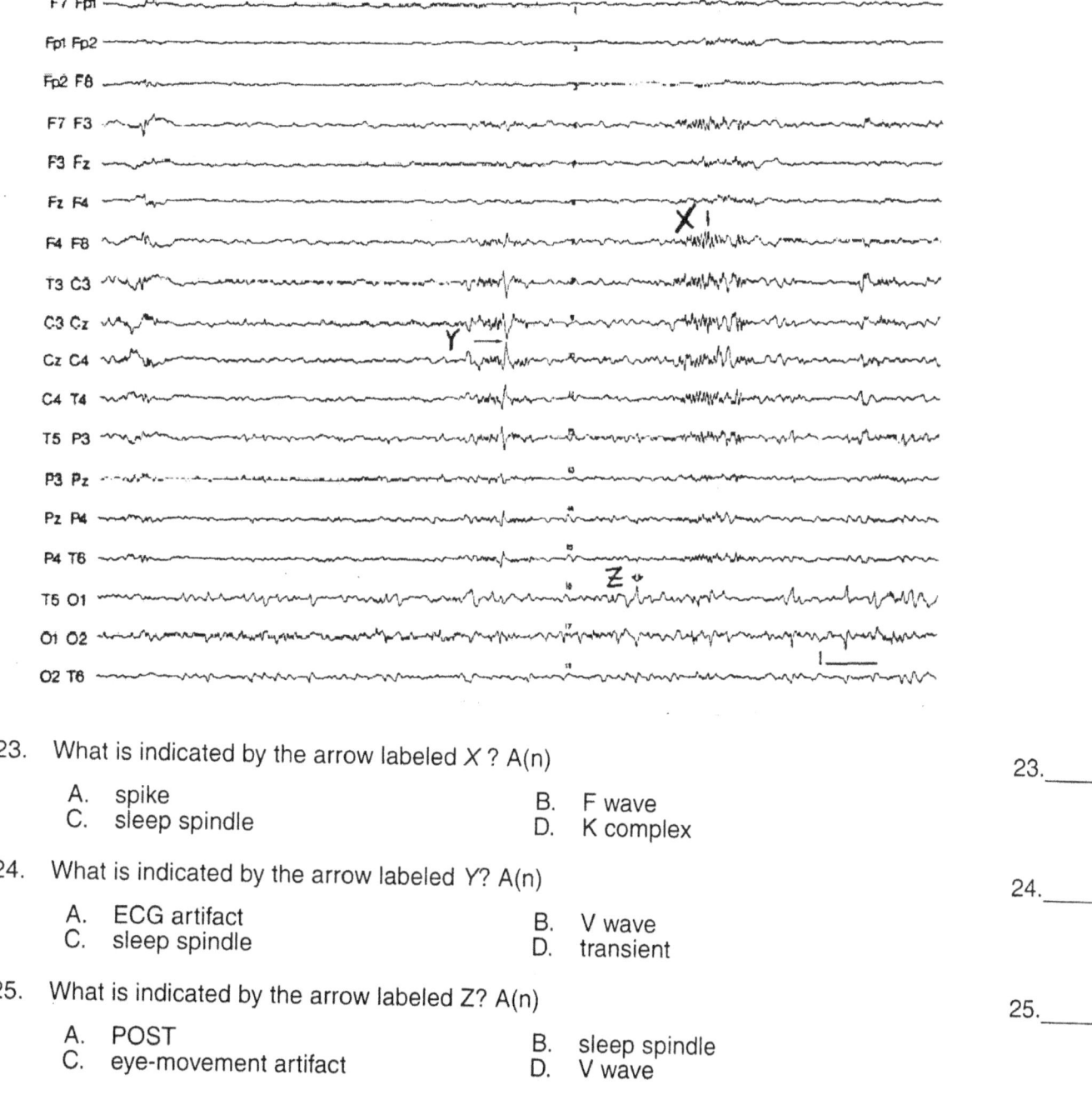

23. What is indicated by the arrow labeled X? A(n)

    A. spike
    B. F wave
    C. sleep spindle
    D. K complex

23._____

24. What is indicated by the arrow labeled Y? A(n)

    A. ECG artifact
    B. V wave
    C. sleep spindle
    D. transient

24._____

25. What is indicated by the arrow labeled Z? A(n)

    A. POST
    B. sleep spindle
    C. eye-movement artifact
    D. V wave

25._____

KEY (CORRECT ANSWERS)

1.	C	11.	A
2.	B	12.	C
3.	B	13.	D
4.	A	14.	B
5.	A	15.	B
6.	B	16.	B
7.	B	17.	A
8.	B	18.	C
9.	A	19.	B
10.	B	20.	B

21. D
22. C
23. C
24. B
25. A

TEST 2

DIRECTIONS: Each question or incomplete statement is followed by several suggested answers or completions. Select the one that BEST answers the question or completes the statement. *PRINT THE LETTER OF THE CORRECT ANSWER IN THE SPACE AT THE RIGHT.*

1. A technician discovers an aberrant signal on a single channel of the chart while an EEG is being taken, and switches the machine over to calibration to observe it more closely. When the machine is switched over to calibration, however, the strange signal disappears and the channel calibrates properly.
   In order to investigate the source of this signal, the technician should

   A. check the external environment for interference
   B. use substitution on the channel's amplifier
   C. test the channel electrode in a different input board jack
   D. switch to a bipolar montage

2. Which of the following electrodes is NOT in the frontal coronal row?

   A. Fz   B. F2   C. F3   D. F4

3. According to the American EEG Society's recommendations, the high-frequency filter for standard recordings should be NO lower than _____ Hz.

   A. 10   B. 30   C. 70   D. 140

4. When an EEG machine's master writer switch is in the chart position,

   A. electronic portions of the machine are on and the chart paper runs through the machine
   B. the amplifier outputs are connected to the pen motors so that the EEGs are traced out on the moving chart
   C. the chart drive is engaged, but the all-channel control circuit is off
   D. electronic portions of the machine are on, but the chart drive does not operate

5. Occasionally, an increase in the amplitude and abundance of EEG alpha activity occurs with a patient's attention or eye opening.
   This condition is known as

   A. synchrony   B. the paradoxical effect
   C. phase reversal   D. diffusion

6. Which of the following is NOT a type of neuron found in the cerebral cortex?

   A. Stellate   B. Elongated   C. Pyramidal   D. Spindle

7. What term is commonly used to denote a particular but arbitrarily selected interval of time in an EEG tracing?

   A. Frequency   B. Period   C. Term   D. Epoch

8. When input voltages of opposite polarities are connected to grids 1 and 2 of a differential amplifier, _____ occurs.

   A. cancellation   B. digital subtraction
   C. summation   D. true phase reversal

9. At a frequency of 95 Hz, the amplitude of most EEG machines will be reduced by approximately _____ %,

   A. 10   B. 25   C. 50   D. 65

10. During which stage of sleep will sleep spindles generally disappear from an EEG?

    A. II   B. III   C. IV   D. REM

11. In establishing the positions of electrodes placed along the circumference of the head, which of the following steps would be performed LAST?

    A. Moving backward from the 5% point, mark the anterior temporal position
    B. Recording head circumference
    C. Verifying 10% distance between occipital positions and left and right side
    D. Drawing a horizontal mark through the 5% point

12. Which of the following is a condition of a subject's photomyogenic response to photic stimuli during EEG recording?

    A. Tonic-clonic seizure or myoclonic jerks
    B. Generalized cortical location
    C. Independent of flash frequency
    D. Muscle-spike morphology

Question 13.

DIRECTIONS: Question 13 refers to the figure shown on the following page, a diagram of an 18-channel EEG.

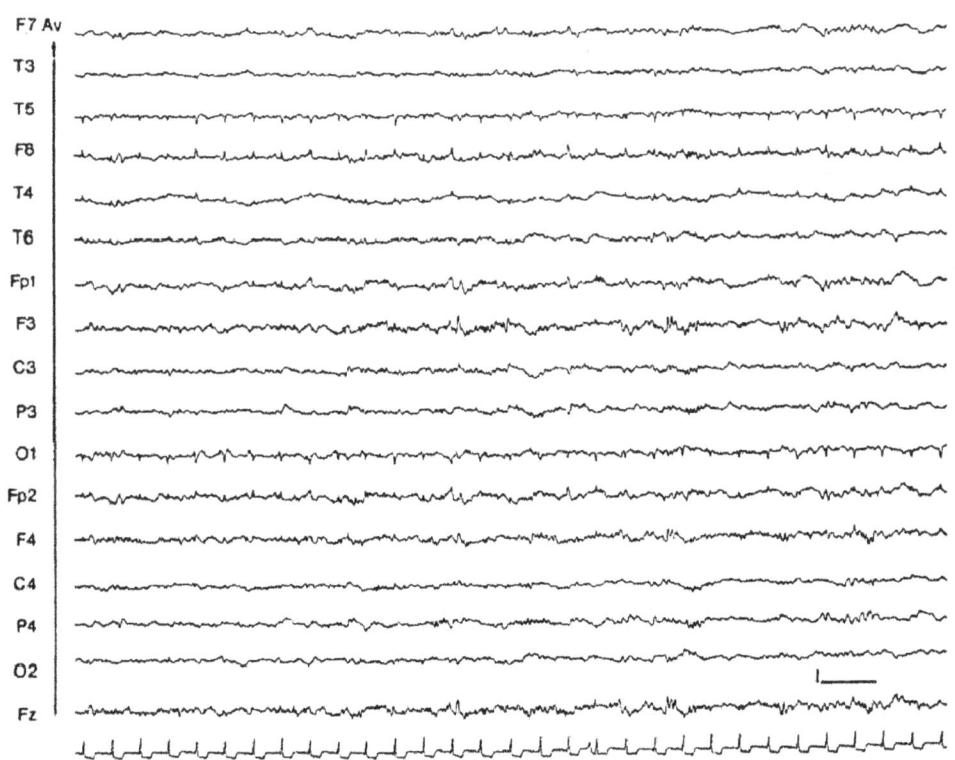

13. What is indicated by the EEG in the figure? 13.____

    A. Diffuse beta activity
    B. Mild epileptiform activity
    C. Normal Stage II sleep
    D. An ECG artifact

14. To protect the patient from hazardous currents flowing between two points, a special electrode board is sometimes used in which a current-limiting solid-state component is connected in series with each of the leads that are attached to the patient's head. This device is known as a(n) 14.____

    A. bipotential isolator   B. leakage current
    C. isoground   D. ground loop

15. According to the American EEG Society's recommendation, inter-electrode impedance, checked prior to recording, should NOT exceed _____ ft. 15.____

    A. 5   B. 40   C. 540   D. 10,000

16. To determine if a breakdown is attributable to the all-channel control circuit, a technician should FIRST 16.____

    A. short-circuit the all-control channel circuit
    B. check the fuses of the all-control channel circuit
    C. measure the voltage feeding the calibration circuit
    D. set all amplifiers for independent channel control

17. EEG activity that is present on only one side of the head is described as 17.____

    A. transverse   B. coronal
    C. lateralized   D. split-brained

18. Which type of electrode is used specifically for recording activity from the basal cortex? 18.____

    A. Sphenoidal   B. Needle
    C. Zygomatic   D. Subdural

Question 19.

DIRECTIONS: Question 19 refers to the figure below, a diagram of an 18-channel EEG recorded during sleep.

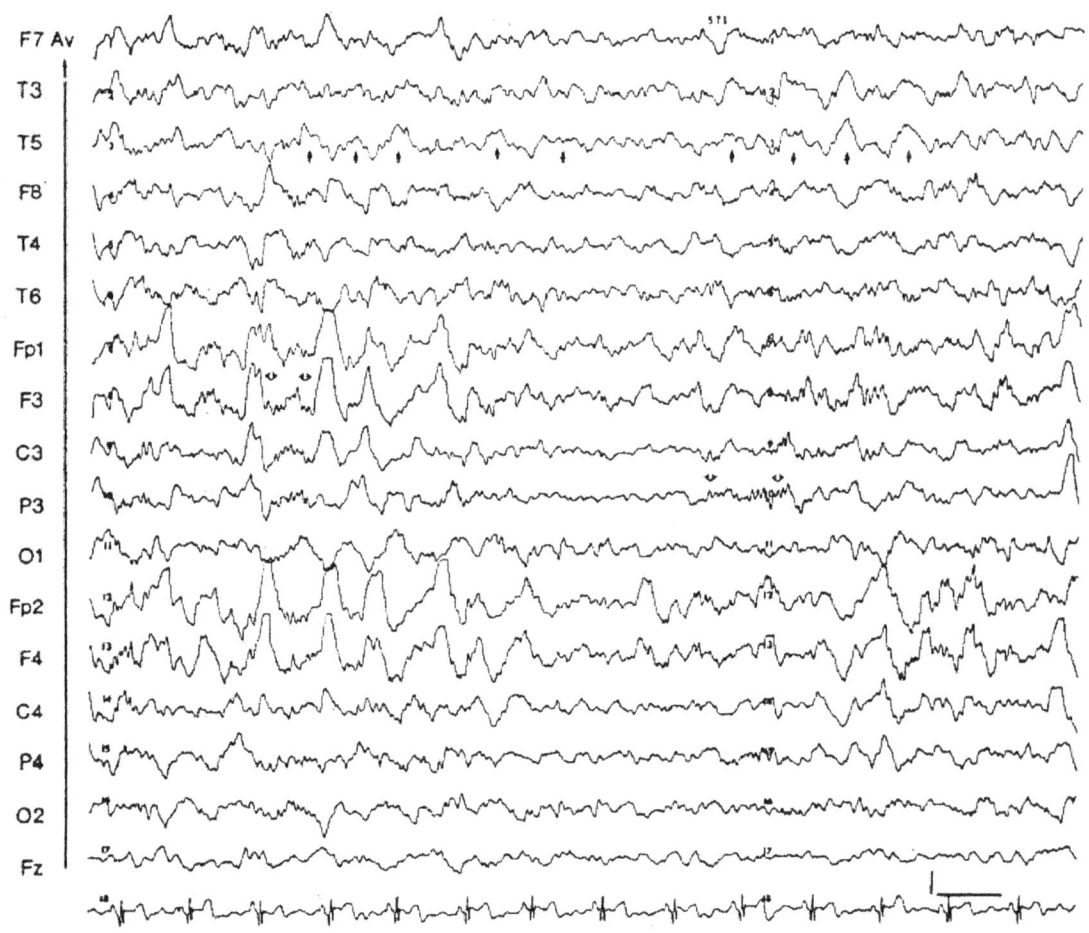

19. What stage of sleep is recorded in the EEC in the figure? 19.___

    A. I B. II C. III D. IV

20. In EEG applications, what is the term for a current that passes from an external surface area of the body to another, and is perceptible to the person exposed to it? 20.___

    A. Infarction B. Macroshock
    C. Spindle D. Microshock

Question 21.

DIRECTIONS: Question 21 refers to the information below: four representations of EEG montages labeled 1, 2, 3, and 4. Study each montage and then answer Question 21.

CHANNEL NO.	MONTAGE #1	MONTAGE #2	MONTAGE #3	MONTAGE #4
1	Fz-Al	Fpl-F7	Fpl-Fp2	Fz-Cz
2	Pz-A2	F7-T3	F7-F3	Cz-Pz
3	Fpl-Al	T3-T5	F3-Fz	Fpl-F7
4	Fp2-A2	T5-01	Fz-F4	F7-T3
5	F3-A1	Fp2-F8	F4-F8	T3-T5
6	F4-A2	F8-T4	A1-T3	T5-01
7	C3-A1	T4-T6	T3-C3	Fp2-F8
8	C4-A2	T6-02	C3-Cz	F8-T4
9	P3-A1	Fz-Cz	Cz-C4	T4-T6
10	P4-A2	Cz-Pz	C4-T4	T6-02
11	01-A1		T4-A2	
12	02-A2		T5-P3	
13	F7-A1		P3-Pz	
14	F8-A2		Pz-P4	
15	T3-A1		P4-T6	
16	T4-A2		01-02	
17	T5-A1		Fz-Cz	
18	T6-A2		Cz-Pz	

21. Which of the montages above is a *referential* montage?

    A. 1   B. 2   C. 3   D. 4

22. What is the term for a particular pair of neurons connected to a single amplifier?

    A. Lead   B. Montage   C. Polarity   D. Derivation

23. According to the American EEG Society's recommendations, the baseline record of an EEG should contain AT LEAST _____ minutes of technically satisfactory recording.

    A. 10   B. 20   C. 45   D. 60

24. In establishing the locations of all 19 scalp electrodes, which of the following electrodes is generally marked FIRST?

    A. Fpz   B. TI   C. Cz   D. Fpl

25. What is the term for a sequence of two or more waves that occur together and repeat at fairly constant intervals?

    A. Structure   B. System   C. Complex   D. Cluster

KEY (CORRECT ANSWERS)

1.	D	11.	D
2.	B	12.	D
3.	C	13.	D
4.	A	14.	A
5.	B	15.	A
6.	B	16.	D
7.	D	17.	C
8.	C	18.	A
9.	C	19.	C
10.	C	20.	B

21. A
22. D
23. B
24. A
25. C

EXAMINATION SECTION
TEST 1

DIRECTIONS: Each question or incomplete statement is followed by several suggested answers or completions. Select the one that BEST answers the question or completes the statement. *PRINT THE LETTER OF THE CORRECT ANSWER IN THE SPACE AT THE RIGHT.*

Question 1.

DIRECTIONS: Question 1 refers to the figure below, a diagram of an 18-channel EEG.

1. The bold arrows in the figure indicate 1.____

   A. yawn artifacts
   B. eye-movement artifacts
   C. muscle spikes
   D. V waves

2. What is the term for a filter that selectively attenuates a very narrow frequency band? 2.____

   A. Osmotic filter
   B. Chooser
   C. Notch filter
   D. Low-pass filter

3. The gain control switch of an EEG machine controls the 3.____

   A. input voltage
   B. chart drive speed

C. deflection sensitivity of the channels
D. output voltage

4. What is the MAXIMUM allowable leakage current (yA) between the electrodes and ground of an EEG machine?

   A. 25   B. 50   C. 70   D. 100

5. Round or flat connector plug ends are MOST effectively cleaned with

   A. emery cloth
   B. alcohol and a cotton swab
   C. a rounded pencil eraser
   D. a small flat file

6. Vertex waves are a feature of an EEG that are MOST prominent in

   A. stage II sleep
   B. tonic-clonic seizure episodes
   C. cerebrovascular disorders
   D. a state of relaxed wakefulness

7. In establishing the positions of electrodes placed along the left and right parasagittal rows, which of the following steps would be performed FIRST?

   A. Define parietal regions
   B. Measure distance from Fp1 to 01
   C. Establish position of C3 and C4 electrodes
   D. Locate frontal region with mark that is 25% backward from Fpl

8. Each of the following EEG components has a common relationship with all the channels in use EXCEPT

   A. electrode board   B. calibrator
   C. power supply   D. all-channel control circuit

9. What is the term for the electrode landmark that is located at the protrusion or bump at the back of the head?

   A. Inion   B. Pre-auricular point
   C. Occipital bun   D. Nasion

Questions 10-15.

DIRECTIONS: Questions 10 through 15 refer to the figure below, a median diagram of the human brain. Place the number that corresponds to each component in the space at the right next to the component's name.

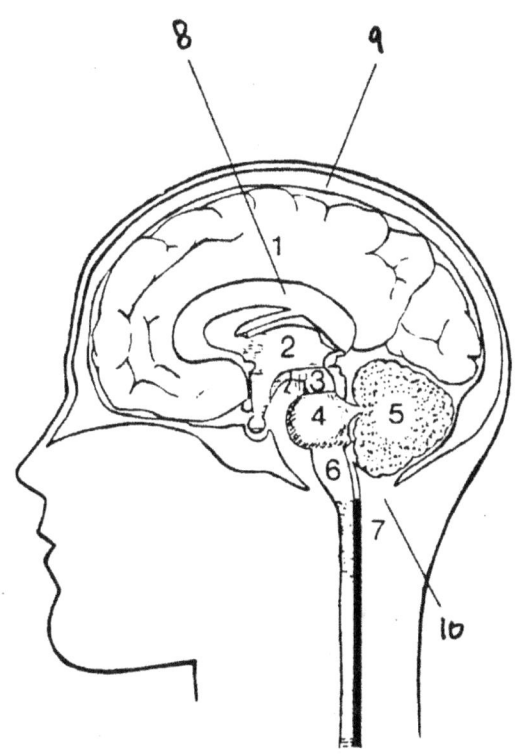

10. Cerebellum 10.____

11. Diencephalon 11.____

12. Cerebral hemisphere 12.____

13. Pons 13.____

14. Medulla oblongata 14.____

15. Midbrain 15.____

16. Which type of electrode is used specifically for recording activity from the orbitofrontal cortex? 16.____

    A. Nasopharyngeal   B. Zygomatic
    C. Cup   D. Ethmoidal

17. Approximately how many meters of recording chart will be used during a 30-minute EEG recording at 30 mm/sec? 17.____

    A. 12   B. 36   C. 54   D. 72

18. K complex 18.____

    A. is commonly diphasic
    B. can occur spontaneously
    C. is a slow-wave transient
    D. is not usually a feature of REM sleep

19. Which of the following electrodes is known as the frontal pole?

    A. Fp1   B. Cz   C. Fpz   D. P1

20. When photic stimulation is used for EEG purposes, _____ flashes are commonly thought to be most effective in stimulating photoparoxysmal responses.

    A. infrared
    B. white
    C. ultraviolet
    D. red

21. What is the term for a group of rhythmic waves in which there is a gradual increase and then a decrease in voltage?

    A. Complex   B. Spindle   C. Sinusoid   D. Spike

22. What is the term for the complete sequence of potential changes undergone by a wave before the sequence is repeated?

    A. String   B. Run   C. Complex   D. Cycle

23. Electrode-board artifacts in an EEG are generally the result of

    A. intermittent single-channel malfunction
    B. paste or prep material on the plug end of an electrode
    C. faulty contact in the connector of the interconnecting cable
    D. salt bridges

24. A group of rhythmic waves in which there is a gradual increase and then a decrease in amplitude is known as a

    A. spindle
    B. run
    C. mu rhythm
    D. sharp wave

25. In an EEG tracing, extreme flat-topped pen excursions, sometimes lasting several seconds, appear. This is probably a manifestation of

    A. clipping
    B. amplifier blocking
    C. cancellation
    D. F wave

KEY (CORRECT ANSWERS)

1. B
2. C
3. C
4. B
5. C

6. A
7. B
8. A
9. A
10. 5

11. 2
12. 1
13. 4
14. 6
15. 3

16. D
17. C
18. D
19. C
20. D

21. B
22. D
23. B
24. A
25. D

TEST 2

DIRECTIONS: Each question or incomplete statement is followed by several suggested answers or completions. Select the one that BEST answers the question or completes the statement. *PRINT THE LETTER OF THE CORRECT ANSWER IN THE SPACE AT THE RIGHT.*

Question 1.

DIRECTIONS: Question 1 refers to the figure below, a diagram of an 18-channel EEG.

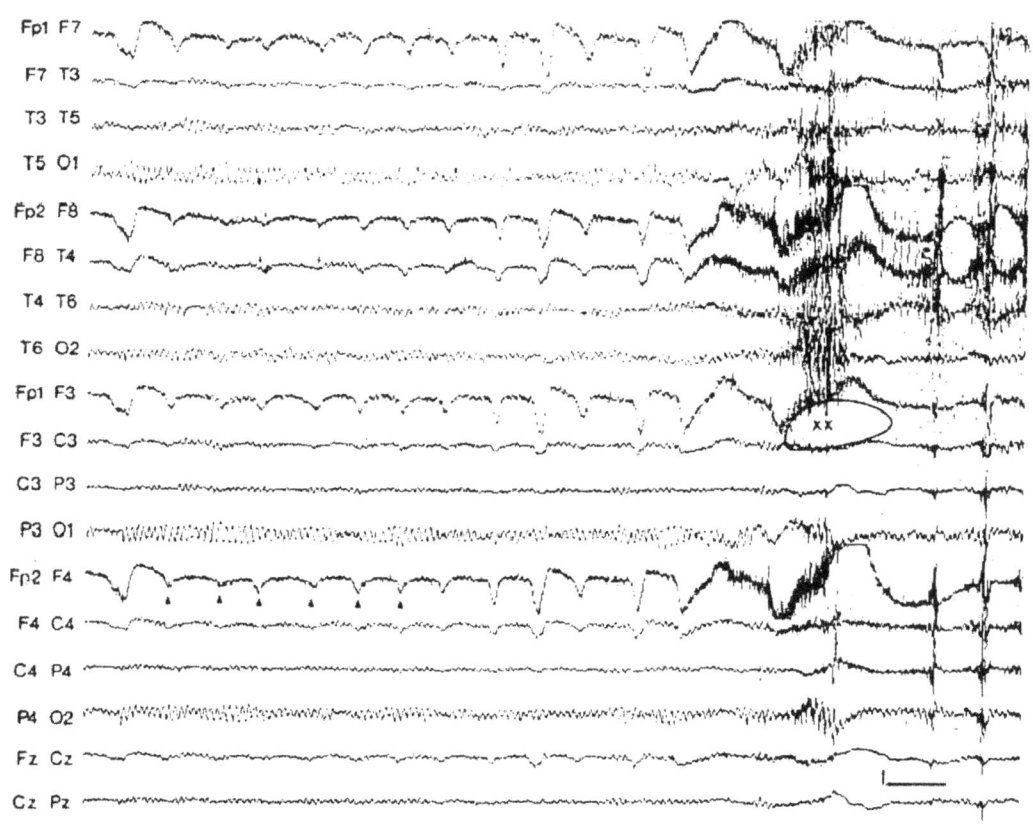

1. What is indicated by the mark *XX* in the EEG in the figure? A(n)

   A. swallowing artifact   B. F wave
   C. yawn artifact   D. K complex

   1.___

2. _____ -wave activity generally comprises more than 50% of an EEG recording during stage IV sleep.

   A. Alpha   B. Beta   C. Delta   D. Theta

   2.___

3. The GREATEST possible risk to a patient who is having an EEG taken occurs when

   A. other electrical devices besides the EEG machine are connected to the patient at the same time
   B. the patient's body touches the chassis of the EEG machine

   3.___

C. any of the electrodes attached to the patient's scalp suddenly acquires a voltage other than voltages derived from the patient
   D. the machine chassis is grounded to copper poles sunk external to the building

4. When input voltages of the same polarity are connected to grids 1 and 2 of a differential amplifier, _____ occurs.

   A. cancellation
   B. digital subtraction
   C. summation
   D. instrumental phase reversal

5. In establishing the positions of electrodes placed along the circumference of the head, which of the following steps would be performed FIRST?

   A. Drawing a horizontal mark through the 5% point
   B. Lining tape up with frontal pole
   C. Moving backward from the 5% point, mark the anterior temporal position
   D. Verifying 10% distance between occipital positions and left and right side

6. The negative pole or electrode of a battery is the

   A. anode   B. dielectric   C. cathode   D. dipole

7. Which of the following is a condition of a subject's photoparoxysmal response to photic stimuli during EEG recording?

   A. Often outlasts duration of photic stimulation
   B. Contraction of facial muscles synchronous with flash
   C. Frontal and frontopolar cortical location
   D. Frequency follows flash frequency

8. POSTS in an EEG occur are typically a feature of

   A. drowsiness
   B. dementia
   C. milder epileptiform activity
   D. stage II sleep

9. What is the PRIMARY advantage associated with EEG machines using a separate ink-well for each pen?

   A. Greater recording accuracy
   B. Lesser likelihood of write malfunction
   C. Greater pen pressure adjustability
   D. Easier filling

10. The electronic portions of an EEC machine are on, but the chart drive is not operating. Assuming that the main power switch is on, what position is the master writer switch in?

    A. On   B. Off   C. Chart   D. Run

11. Overload may cause distortion of EEG waves, making them appear flat-topped in the write-out.
    This distortion is known as

    A. asymmetry   B. clipping
    C. mu rhythm   D. chopping

12. The input voltage (μv) on grid 1 of an EEG's differential amplifier is 100; and the input voltage for grid 2 is 75. The output voltage will be _____ μv.

    A. -25   B. 25   C. -175   D. 175

13. Artifacts in an EEG are known to be caused by a single-channel malfunction that has spread to other channels. Which of the following components should be checked FIRST?

    A. Amplifier connector   B. All-channel control
    C. Amplifier   D. Input board

14. According to the American EEG Society's recommendations, the low-frequency filter for standard recordings should be no higher than _____ Hz.

    A. 0.5   B. 1   C. 5   D. 10

15. Calibrator artifacts in an EEG MOST often occur as

    A. rhythmic flattening of a single channel
    B. an apparent isoelectric record
    C. rhythmic flattening of waves having the same pattern in all channels
    D. intermittent, randomly occurring spikes having the same pattern in all channels

16. In EEG applications, what is the term for a very small current that pass into the interior of the body through indwelling electrodes, catheters, or implanted transducers?

    A. Infarction   B. Macroshock
    C. Spike   D. Microshock

Questions 17-19.

DIRECTIONS: Questions 17 through 19 refer to the figure below, a diagram of an 18-channel EEG.

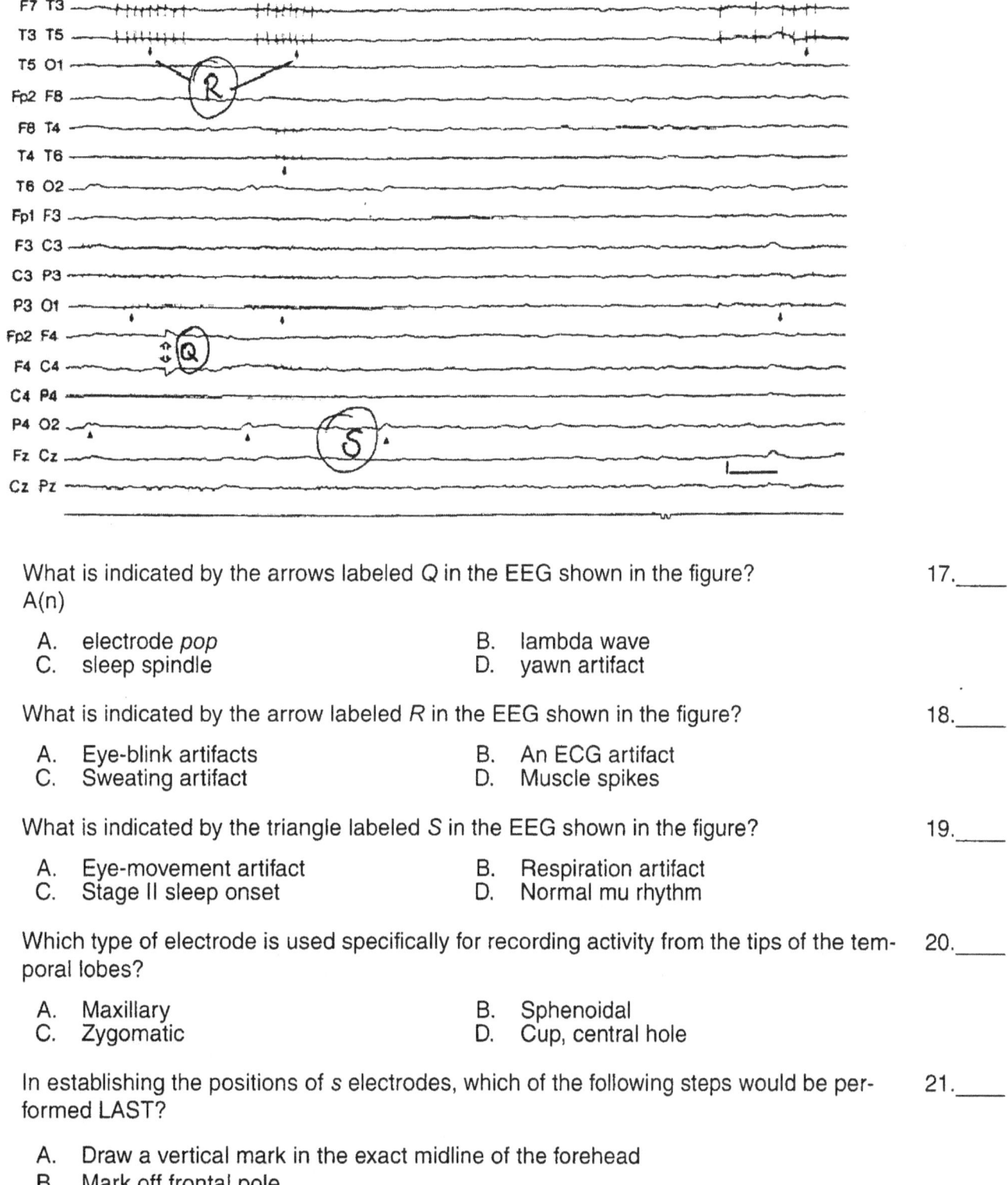

17. What is indicated by the arrows labeled Q in the EEG shown in the figure? A(n)

    A. electrode *pop*
    B. lambda wave
    C. sleep spindle
    D. yawn artifact

18. What is indicated by the arrow labeled R in the EEG shown in the figure?

    A. Eye-blink artifacts
    B. An ECG artifact
    C. Sweating artifact
    D. Muscle spikes

19. What is indicated by the triangle labeled S in the EEG shown in the figure?

    A. Eye-movement artifact
    B. Respiration artifact
    C. Stage II sleep onset
    D. Normal mu rhythm

20. Which type of electrode is used specifically for recording activity from the tips of the temporal lobes?

    A. Maxillary
    B. Sphenoidal
    C. Zygomatic
    D. Cup, central hole

21. In establishing the positions of s electrodes, which of the following steps would be performed LAST?

    A. Draw a vertical mark in the exact midline of the forehead
    B. Mark off frontal pole
    C. Measure distance from nasion to inion
    D. Mark off occipital region

22. Typically, the ground electrode is attached between electrodes 22.___

    A. O1 and O2 B. Fp1 and Fp2
    C. C3 and C4 D. A1 and A2

Question 23.

DIRECTIONS: Question 23 refers to the information below: four representations of EEG montages labeled 1, 2, 3, and 4. Study each montage and then answer Question 23.

CHANNEL NO.	MONTAGE #1	MONTAGE #2	MONTAGE #3	MONTAGE #4
1	F7-Fp1	F7-A1	Fz-Cz	F7-F3
2	Fp1-Fp2	T3-A1	Cz-Pz	F3-Fz
3	Fp2-F8	T5-A1	Fpl-F3	Fz-F4
4	F7-F3	Fp1-A1	F3-C3	F4-F8
5	F3-Fz	F3-A1	C3-P3	A1-T3
6	Fz-F4	C3-A1	P3-O1	T3-C3
7	F4-F8	P3-A1	Fp2-F4	C3-Cz
8	T3-C3	O1-A1	F4-C4	Cz-C4
9	C3-Cz	Fz-A1	C4-P4	C4-T4
10	Cz-C4	Pz-A2	P4-O2	T4-A2
11	C4-T4	Fp2-A2		
12	T5-P3	F4-A2		
13	P3-Pz	C4-A2		
14	Pz-P4	P4-A2		
15	P4-T6	O2-A2		
16	T5-O1	F8-A2		
17	O1-O2	T4-A2		
18	O2-T6	T6-A2		

23. Which of the montages above is a longitudinal bipolar montage? 23.___

    A. 1 B. 2 C. 3 D. 4

24. What is the specific term for an isolated EEG wave that stands out from the background activity, and has a duration of 70-200 ms? 24.___

    A. Spike   B. Complex
    C. Spindle D. Sharp wave

25. What is the term for the electrode landmark that is located in front of the ear? 25.___

    A. Temporal notch B. Pre-auricular point
    C. Inion   D. Zygoma

KEY (CORRECT ANSWERS)

1. C
2. C
3. A
4. A
5. B

6. C
7. A
8. D
9. B
10. B

11. B
12. D
13. B
14. B
15. D

16. D
17. A
18. D
19. B
20. C

21. A
22. B
23. C
24. D
25. B

EXAMINATION SECTION
TEST 1

DIRECTIONS: Each question or incomplete statement is followed by several suggested answers or completions. Select the one the BEST answers the question or completes the statement. *PRINT THE LETTER OF THE CORRECT ANSWER IN THE SPACE AT THE RIGHT.*

1. Which of the following symptoms is NOT consistent with normal pressure hydrocephalus?   1.____

   A. Gait disturbance
   B. Urinary incontinence
   C. Tachycardia
   D. Dementia

2. A 46-year-old woman, recently recovered from an upper respiratory infection, reports recent problems with vertigo, nausea, vomiting, and nystagmus. The symptoms have persisted for four days. The most likely disorder is   2.____

   A. vestibular neuritis
   B. cerebral aneurysm
   C. Guillain-Barre syndrome
   D. acoustic neuroma

3. An elderly man has fallen several times in the past few years, but has remained stable and never lost consciousness. He has recently developed increasing mental confusion associated with mild right hemiparesis, and a scan demonstrates compression in the left hemisphere. These findings are most consistent with   3.____

   A. hypertensive hemorrhage
   B. chronic subdural hematoma
   C. Alzheimer's disease
   D. epidural hematoma

4. Neuroreceptors are typically classified according to the   4.____

   A. frequency of their response to a stimulus
   B. type of stimulus they convert
   C. type of signal they produce
   D. speed with which they respond to a stimulus

5. Somatosensory input is received and interpreted by the brain's _____ lobe.   5.____

   A. frontal
   B. parietal
   C. temporal
   D. occipital

6. Treatments of Gullain-Barre syndrome include
   I. Early plasmapharesis
   II. Immunoglobulin infusion
   III. Orthotics
   IV. Tricyclic antidepressant medications

   A. I and II
   B. I, III and IV
   C. II only
   D. I, II, III and IV

7. Which of the following statements about neurons with a myelin sheath is TRUE?

   A. They transmit nerve impulses rapidly.
   B. They consist of multiple cell bodies.
   C. Once an axon is damaged, it can't be repaired.
   D. Neurotransmitters may be involved in transmitting a message, but are not required.

8. Which of the following is consistent with a stroke involving the left posterior cerebellar artery?

   A. diplopia
   B. uniform visual hallucinations
   C. memory impairment
   D. aphasia

9. Which of the following is LEAST likely to be involved in a cran-iopharyngioma?

   A. hypothalamus
   B. optic nerve
   C. third ventricle
   D. pituitary gland

10. The pons and reticular formation are found in the

    A. spinal cord
    B. forebrain
    C. midbrain
    D. hindbrain

11. Tricyclic antidepressants effect neurotransmitters during

    A. degradation
    B. storage
    C. reuptake
    D. production

12. Impulses are transmitted by motor neurons

    A. among components of the central nervous system
    B. from stimulus receptors
    C. away from the central nervous system
    D. between the axon bulbs of individual neurons

13. Cubital tunnel syndrome is characterized by each of the following, EXCEPT

    A. weakness in intrinsic hand muscles
    B. parasthesia/numbness in ring finger
    C. negative elbow flexion test
    D. medial elbow pain

14. Which of the following neoplasms is well-differentiated, likely to present with hydrocephalus, and more common in children?

    A. Brain stem glioma
    B. Ependymoma
    C. Choroid plexus papilloma
    D. Meningioma

15. During the _____, an action potential cannot be gener-ated in a neuron.

    A. membrane hyperpolarization
    B. membrane depolarization
    C. relative refractory period
    D. absolute refractory period

16. An electrical synapse is also known as a(n)

    A. ligand-gated channel
    B. voltage-gated channel
    C. gap junction channel
    D. transmitter-gated channel

17. In cases of cerebral edema, the greatest increases in sodium and water content typically occur in the

    A. white matter
    B. meninges
    C. gray matter
    D. dura

18. What is the term for the innermost layer of the meninges?

    A. arachnoid
    B. falx
    C. pia mater
    D. dura mater

19. A 50-year-old man has experienced severe headaches that have wors-ened over the past several weeks, and now has difficulty moving his left arm. He presents papilledema that is worse on the right. The most likely condition to be associated with these findings is

    A. neovascularization around a glioma
    B. HIV encephalopathy
    C. neuronal storage disease
    D. overproduction of cerebrospinal fluid

20. The cerebral lobes primarily involved in planning and performing movement are the _____ lobes.

   A. temporal
   B. parietal
   C. sagittal
   D. frontal

21. A person has lost pain and temperature sensation, but has retained the sensation of touch. A disorder consistent with these findings is

   A. Cerebrovascular accident
   B. Syringomyelia
   C. Subdural hemotoma
   D. Wegener's granulomatosis

22. Which of the following disorders is associated with a reduction in the size of the caudate nuclei?

   A. Parkinson's disease
   B. Huntington's disease
   C. Charcot-Marie-Tooth disease
   D. Amyotrophic lateral sclerosis

23. In the vestibular system, rotations of the head are sensed by the

   A. ipsilateral and contralateral neurons of the brain stem
   B. maculae of the utricle and the saccule
   C. ampullae in the semicircular canals
   D. Y nucleus

24. Typical findings of carpal tunnel syndrome include each of the following, EXCEPT

   A. decreased sensation in the thumb
   B. atrophy of thenar eminence
   C. spasms of the flexor carpi ulnaris
   D. decreased sensation in the index and middle fingers

25. The earliest symptom of acoustic nerve tumors is usually

   A. hemiparesis
   B. vertigo
   C. ataxia
   D. tinnitus

KEY (CORRECT ANSWERS)

1.	C	11.	C
2.	A	12.	C
3.	B	13.	C
4.	B	14.	C
5.	B	15.	D
6.	A	16.	C
7.	A	17.	A
8.	B	18.	C
9.	A	19.	A
10.	D	20.	D

21. B
22. B
23. C
24. C
25. D

TEST 2

DIRECTIONS: Each question or incomplete statement is followed by several suggested answers or completions. Select the one the BEST answers the question or completes the statement. *PRINT THE LETTER OF THE CORRECT ANSWER IN THE SPACE AT THE RIGHT.*

1. Which of the following is a disorder caused by excessive cerebrospinal fluid?

    A. Meningitis
    B. Hydrocephalus
    C. Subdural edema
    D. Pneumoencephalus

2. The main classes of neuroreceptors include each of the following, EXCEPT

    A. photoreceptors
    B. nociceptors
    C. mechanoreceptors
    D. palpireceptors

3. Which of the following is NOT associated with central vertigo?

    A. Multiple sclerosis
    B. Vascular insufficiency
    C. Meniere's disease
    D. Migraine headache

4. A patient has subacute lower back pain, suspected nerve involvement represented by leg pain should be evaluated by means of

    A. CAT scan
    B. electromyelography
    C. knee-jerk reflex test
    D. MRI scan

5. Which of the following are receptor-blocking drugs used to treat the psychotic symptoms of schizophrenia?

    A. Phenothiazines
    B. Menzodiazepines
    C. Oxidase inhibitors
    D. Atropines

6. The main function of the sodium/potassium pump is to

    A. polarize the neuron
    B. release neurotransmitter
    C. maintain cell volume
    D. decode the strength of a stimulus

7. Which of the following neoplasms is likely to be located in the 4th ventricle in childhood, or in the spinal cord in adults?

    A. Oligodendroglioma
    B. Ependymoma
    C. Glioblastoma
    D. Astrocytoma

8. Major causes of dementia include
    I. cephalic disorders
    II. Alzheimer's disease
    III. multi-infarct
    IV. metabolic disorders

    A. I and II
    B. II and III
    C. II and IV
    D. I, II, III and IV

9. Tay-Sachs disease is associated with a decrease in

    A. gamma globulin
    B. sphingomyelinase
    C. hexosaminidase A
    D. glucocerebrosidase

10. Which of the following areas would NOT be involved in a basilar artery stroke?

    A. Pons
    B. Midbrain
    C. Basal ganglia
    D. Occipital cortex

11. A seizure lasting more than 10 minutes, or a second seizure prior to regaining consciousness from a first seizure, is defined as

    A. generalized
    B. tonic-clonic
    C. complex partial
    D. status epilepticus

12. Common symptoms of frontal lobe tumors include
    I. hemiplegia
    II. seizures
    III. memory deficit
    IV. speech disturbances

    A. I only
    B. I, II and III
    C. II, III and IV
    D. I, II, III and IV

13. Berry aneurysms occur at the

    A. lacunae
    B. posterior pericallosal artery
    C. basilar artery
    D. bifurcation of the Circle of Willis

14. Of the following conditions, which is LEAST likely to obstruct the flow of cerebrospinal fluid and cause ventricular enlargement?

    A. pneumococcal meningitis
    B. epidural hematoma
    C. forking in the aqueduct of Sylvius
    D. intraventricular hemorrhage

15. The lateral geniculate is a thalamic nucleus involved in

    A. vision
    B. hearing
    C. taste
    D. smell

16. Gangliogliomas are rare neoplasms that usually affect the _____ lobes of the cerebral hemispheres.

    A. frontal
    B. temporal
    C. parietal
    D. occipital

17. A hemorrhage involving the region of the right basal ganglia is most likely to develop as a result of

    A. severe trauma
    B. vascular malformation
    C. hypertension
    D. encephalitis

18. Most motor neurons are stimulated by

    A. mechanoreceptors
    B. sensory neurons
    C. glands
    D. interneurons

19. A 53-year-old woman has diabetes mellitus. Which of the following is LEAST likely to be associated with her peripheral neuropathy?

    A. Symmetrical involvement
    B. More severe effect on axons than dendrites
    C. More severe effect on motor nerves than sensory nerves
    D. More severe effect on distal nerves in the extremities

20. Electrochemical equilibrium refers to the balance between _____ force and _____ force.

    A. nuclear; inertial
    B. electrostatic; diffusion
    C. molecular; electromagnetic
    D. frictional; gravitational

21. The brain's third ventricle is surrounded by the

    A. hypothalamus
    B. thalamus
    C. aqueduct of Sylvius
    D. pons

22. A neurons action potential
    I. appears on the cell body membrane
    II. is "all-or-none"
    III. is self-generating
    IV. uses volt-sensitive ion channels

    A. I and IV
    B. I, II and III
    C. II, III and IV
    D. I, II, III and IV

23. Rods and cones are examples of
    I. chemoreceptors
    II. proprioceptors
    III. photoreceptors
    IV. exteroceptors

    A. I only
    B. I and II
    C. III only
    D. III and IV

24. The cerebellum negotiates

    A. emotions
    B. somatosensory input
    C. speech
    D. motor coordination

25. Causes of sensorineural hearing loss include
    I. congenital
    II. Meniere's disease
    III. aging
    IV. acoustic injury

    A. I only
    B. I, III and IV
    C. II and III
    D. I, II, III and IV

KEY (CORRECT ANSWERS)

1.	B	11.	D
2.	D	12.	B
3.	C	13.	D
4.	B	14.	A
5.	A	15.	A
6.	C	16.	B
7.	B	17.	C
8.	B	18.	D
9.	C	19.	C
10.	C	20.	B

21. B
22. C
23. C
24. D
25. D

TEST 3

DIRECTIONS: Each question or incomplete statement is followed by several suggested answers or completions. Select the one the BEST answers the question or completes the statement. *PRINT THE LETTER OF THE CORRECT ANSWER IN THE SPACE AT THE RIGHT.*

1. The frequency of "treatable" causes of dementia is estimated to be about _____ %.   1.____

    A. 20
    B. 40
    C. 60
    D. 80

2. Which of the following is NOT a type of glioma?   2.____

    A. Ependymoma
    B. Astrocytoma
    C. Oligodendroglioma
    D. Chordoma

3. The central nervous system interprets impulses based on their frequency and   3.____

    A. origin
    B. speed
    C. type
    D. duration

4. The ion responsible for the reversal of membrane potential during the action potential is   4.____

    A. calcium
    B. chloride
    C. sodium
    D. potassium

5. Which of the following is NOT a common symptom of Horner's syndrome?   5.____

    A. Red, dry skin (anhidrosis)
    B. Drooping eyelid (ptosis)
    C. Tinnitus
    D. Pupil constriction (miosis)

6. Each of the following senses is processed in the thalamus before reaching the cerebral cortex, EXCEPT   6.____

    A. taste
    B. smell
    C. vision
    D. somatosensory

7. Eye movement is governed by which of the following cranial nerves?   7.____

    A. second (optic)
    B. fifth (trigeminal)
    C. sixth (abducent)
    D. eighth (vestibulocochlear)

8. An embolism that causes acute onset of left hemiparesis, facial droop, and occlusion of the right middle cerebral artery has come from the

   A. aortic arch
   B. saphenous vein
   C. carotid bifurcation
   D. left atrium

9. The strength of a stimulus is typically encoded in the

   A. frequency of the action potentials that it generates
   B. voltage of the postsynaptic membrane
   C. number of action potentials that it generates
   D. threshold voltage of the neuron

10. Which of the following neoplasms is ALWAYS located in the cerebellum?

    A. Oligodendroglioma
    B. Meningioma
    C. Schwannoma
    D. Medulloblastoma

11. A seizure that arises in both cerebral hemispheres is described as

    A. complex
    B. febrile
    C. tonic-clonic
    D. generalized

12. Metachromatic leukodystrophy is associated with a deficiency in

    A. myrosinase
    B. glucocerebrosidase
    C. neuraminidase
    D. sphingomyelinase

13. Inhibitory neurotransmitters

    A. raise the threshold voltage of the neuron
    B. open sodium channels in the plasma membrane
    C. hyperpolarize the postsynaptic membrane
    D. depolarize the postsynaptic membrane

14. Dymyelinating diseases include
    I. metachromatic leukodystrophy
    II. postinfectious encephalomyelitis
    III. multiple sclerosis
    IV. progressive multifocal leukoencephalopathy

    A. I and II
    B. I, III and IV
    C. II and III
    D. I, II, III and IV

15. A 50-year-old woman has had a severe headache for several days. A physical exam reveals right-side papilledema, and a head CAT scan reveals a marked right-to-left midline shift. An MRI scan shows a 5 cm enhancing mass lesion in the right parietal region with marked surrounding edema. Which of the following conditions is most likely?

    A. Pontine hemorrhages
    B. Diffuse subarachnoid hemorrhage
    C. Posterior cerebral artery thrombosis
    D. Superior sagittal sinus thrombosis

16. The hemispheres of the cerebrum are separated by the

    A. superior sagittal sinus
    B. falx cerebri
    C. choroid plexus
    D. tentorium cerebri

17. Alzheimer's disease is characterized by each of the following, EXCEPT

    A. Neuritic plaques
    B. Hirano bodies
    C. decreased myelin
    D. decreased numbers of neurons in the nucleus basalis of Meynert

18. What area of the brain is implicated in long-term potentiation?

    A. Hypothalamus
    B. Hippocampus
    C. Amygdala
    D. Pons

19. Axons are specialized structures that are designed to

    A. conduct electrical impulses
    B. interpret electrical messages
    C. generate chemical messages
    D. protect nerve cells

20. Symptoms of a basilar artery stroke include
    I. visual field deficits
    II. quadriparesis
    III. diplopia
    IV. right homonymous hemianopsia

    A. I only
    B. I, II and III
    C. II and III
    D. I, II, III and IV

21. Motor neuron axons travel outward from the spinal cord through the

    A. cauda equina
    B. dorsal root
    C. ventral root
    D. medial root

22. Parietal lobe tumors are most likely to be associated with

    A. a loss of the ability to write (agraphia)
    B. aphasia
    C. ataxia
    D. hemiparesis

23. Which of the following would be sensed by an exteroceptor?

    A. Muscle tension
    B. Smell
    C. Lung inflation
    D. Mechanical pain

24. A stroke involving the right middle cerebral artery is LEAST likely to affect the

    A. basal ganglia
    B. internal brain capsule
    C. parietal cortex
    D. pons

25. Which of the following is LEAST likely to occur as a consequence of severe head trauma?

    A. Cerebral edema
    B. Loss of sense of smell
    C. Subdural hematoma
    D. Cerebral vasculitis

KEY (CORRECT ANSWERS)

1.	A	11.	D
2.	D	12.	B
3.	A	13.	C
4.	C	14.	D
5.	C	15.	A
6.	B	16.	B
7.	C	17.	C
8.	D	18.	B
9.	A	19.	A
10.	D	20.	B

21. C
22. A
23. D
24. D
25. D

EXAMINATION SECTION
TEST 1

DIRECTIONS: Each question or incomplete statement is followed by several suggested answers or completions. Select the one the BEST answers the question or completes the statement. *PRINT THE LETTER OF THE CORRECT ANSWER IN THE SPACE AT THE RIGHT.*

1. A neuron's action potential is usually generated in the

    A. cell body
    B. axon hillock
    C. nucleus
    D. Schwann cell

2. Classical manifestations of neuroleptic malignant syndrome include each of the following, EXCEPT

    A. Resting tremor
    B. Hyperthermia
    C. Hypertonic skeletal muscles
    D. Fluctuating consciousness

3. The basal ganglia regulates _____ functions.

    A. auditory
    B. somatosensory
    C. motor
    D. visual

4. Cluster headaches are characterized by each of the following, EXCEPT

    A. Periorbital pain
    B. Nasal congestion
    C. Photosensitivity
    D. Homolateral redness of eye, nose

5. Somatic neural sensations originate from receptors in

    A. a specific location in the body
    B. muscles
    C. more than one location in the body
    D. tactile zones in the hands and feet

6. A 46-year-old man develops a psychosis and a choreiform movement disorder. The most likely condition is

    A. Creutzfeld-Jakov disease
    B. Alzheimer's disease
    C. Huntington's disease
    D. Multiple sclerosis

7. A child is stillborn at 34 weeks with marked hydrops fetalis, organomegaly, extensive cerebral necrosis, and preventricular calcification. The cause of death was most likely

    A. cytomegalovirus
    B. HIV
    C. Epstein-Barr virus
    D. Herpes simplex virus

8. The ion necessary for the release of a neurotransmitter is

    A. potassium
    B. sodium
    C. chloride
    D. calcium

9. Emotions and problem-solving are associated with the brain's _____ lobes.

    A. frontal
    B. parietal
    C. temporal
    D. occipital

10. The graded potentials of a sensory receptor are collectively as

    A. Excitatory postsynaptic potential (EPSP)
    B. Inhibitory postsynaptic potential (IPSP)
    C. Generator potential
    D. Threshold

11. "Cushing's Triad" refers to three findings consistent with intracranial pressure. Which of the following is NOT one of these findings?

    A. Irregular breathing
    B. Delirium
    C. Hypertension
    D. Bradycardia

12. A 48-year-old man has become comatose. He has right-side papille-dema and cerebellar tonsillar herniation. Which of the following conditions is LEAST likely?

    A. Glioblastoma multiforme
    B. Chronic subdural hematoma
    C. Wernicke's disease
    D. Cerebral abscess

13. The classic set of symptoms of Meniere's disease includes each of the following, EXCEPT

    A. Tinnitus
    B. Hearing loss
    C. Vertigo
    D. Numbness or tingling in the extremities

14. The ventral amygdalofugal pathway carries projections from the amygdala to the cingulate cortex and the

   A. lateral hypothalamus
   B. orbitofrontal cortex
   C. diencephalon
   D. temporal cortex

15. Of the following brain neoplasms, which has the best post-surgical prognosis?

   A. Schwannoma
   B. Medulloblastoma
   C. Glioblastoma multiforme
   D. Astrocytoma

16. A neurotransmitter allows negatively charged chloride ions into the neuron and increases the membrane potential. Which of the following has occurred?

   A. Facilitated diffusion
   B. Inhibitory postsynaptic potential (IPSP)
   C. Excitatory postsynaptic potential (EPSP)
   D. Threshold voltage

17. Which of the following types of brain neoplasms is LEAST common among children?

   A. Medulloblastoma
   B. Ependymoma
   C. Astrocytoma
   D. Meningioma

18. What is the term for a single neuron's transmission of an impulse to many neurons?

   A. Radiation
   B. Refraction
   C. Summation
   D. Divergence

19. Approximately what percentage of cerebrovascular accidents are hemorrhagic?

   A. 20-30
   B. 30-50
   C. 50-70
   D. 70-80

20. Most commonly, subarachnoid hemorrhages occur secondary to

   A. blood dyscrasias and respiratory problems
   B. cerebral neoplasms
   C. acute infection
   D. arteriovenous malformations (AVM) or berry aneurysm rupture

21. Which of the following would be sensed by an interoceptor?

    A. Joint angle
    B. Venous pressure
    C. Thermal pain
    D. Linear acceleration

22. Which of the following is LEAST likely to be associated with Duret hemorrhages of the midbrain and/or the pons subsequent to severe uncal herniation?

    A. Hypertensive hemorrhage
    B. Alzheimer's disease
    C. Severe head trauma
    D. Meningioma

23. The most prominent example of cortical commissural fibers is the

    A. posterior commissure
    B. choroid plexus
    C. corpus callosum
    D. falx cerebri

24. Which of the following disorders is characterized by a loss of myelin in the central nervous system?

    A. Amyotrophic lateral sclerosis (ALS)
    B. Myasthenia gravis (MG)
    C. Charcot-Marie-Tooth (CMT) disease
    D. Multiple sclerosis (MS)

25. Occipital lobe tumors are most likely to be associated with

    A. blindness in one direction (hemianopsia)
    B. loss of a sense of smell (anosmia)
    C. mental or personality changes
    D. memory deficit

KEY (CORRECT ANSWERS)

1.	B	11.	B
2.	A	12.	C
3.	C	13.	D
4.	C	14.	B
5.	C	15.	A
6.	C	16.	B
7.	A	17.	D
8.	D	18.	D
9.	A	19.	A
10.	C	20.	D

21. B
22. B
23. C
24. D
25. A

TEST 2

DIRECTIONS: Each question or incomplete statement is followed by several suggested answers or completions. Select the one the BEST answers the question or completes the statement. *PRINT THE LETTER OF THE CORRECT ANSWER IN THE SPACE AT THE RIGHT.*

1. The majority of the brain is made up of

   A. sensory neurons
   B. motor neurons
   C. somatosensory receptors
   D. interneurons

2. Each of the following types of seizures involves an alteration of consciousness, EXCEPT

   A. complex partial   B. absence
   C. simple partial   D. temporal lobe

3. If a patient's history and physical examination reveal a significant chance that headache symptoms are secondary to a brain stem lesion, the most appropriate diagnostic tool is

   A. MRI scan
   B. electromyelography
   C. CAT scan
   D. Rorschach test

4. What is the term for the mechanoreceptors of the ear?

   A. Hair cells
   B. Cochlear cells
   C. Proprioceptors
   D. Vestibular cells

5. The origins of the 5th, 6th, 7th, and 8th cranial nerves are contained within the

   A. pons   B. cerebellum
   C. medulla oblongata D. limbic system

6. "Silent" brain tumors – those presenting no symptoms – are most likely to arise in the _____ lobe.

   A. frontal   B. parietal   C. temporal   D. occipital

7. Which of the following is NOT a part of the limbic system?

   A. Substantia nigra   B. Cingulate gyrus
   C. Amygdala   D. Septum

8. Bell's palsy is a neurological disorder caused by damage to the

   A. fourth cranial (trochlear) nerve
   B. sixth cranial (abducent) nerve
   C. seventh cranial (facial) nerve
   D. eighth cranial (vestibulocochlear) nerve

9. A 30-year old man suffers an acute onset of confusion, followed by a seizure. A CAT scan reveals lesion in the left temporal lobe. The findings are most likely to be associated with

   A. astrocytoma
   B. papovavirus
   C. herpes simplex virus
   D. berry aneurysm

10. A proprioceptor is capable of sensing

    A. taste
    B. arterial blood pressure
    C. muscle tension
    D. hair movement

11. A 41-year old woman reports difficulty chewing and swallowing, along with fatigue that worsens with exercise and improves with rest. She presents with drooping eyelids. These findings are consistent with

    A. Guillain-Barre syndrome
    B. myasthenia gravis
    C. neurofibromatosis
    D. fibromyalgia

12. Each of the following is associated with degenerative neurologic diseases, EXCEPT

    A. lack of targeted or curative treatments
    B. worsening neurologic deficits over many years
    C. acute symptoms from a mass effect
    D. loss of specific neuronal groups

13. During impulse transmission, the voltage-gated sodium channels of myelinated neurons are confined to

    A. Schwann cells
    B. the axon hillock
    C. nodes of Ranvier
    D. excitatory synapses

14. The release of acetylcholine can be inhibited by introducing the toxin

    A. botulin   B. tetanus   C. globulin   D. selenium

15. Which of the following is MOST likely to be found with a fast-growing left hemispheric glioma?

    A. Subdural hematoma
    B. Basal ganglia hemorrhage
    C. Pontine Duret hemorrhage
    D. Subarachnoid hemorrhage

16. Sulci

    A. separate the cerebrum from the cerebellum
    B. are furrows in the cerebral cortex
    C. line the cerebral ventricles
    D. are fluids in the inner ear

17. Approximately what percentage of patients with multiple sclerosis will develop optic neuritis?

    A. 20   B. 40   C. 60   D. 80

18. Which of the following types of brain neoplasms is LEAST common among adults?

    A. Ependymoma
    B. Glioblastoma multiforme
    C. Metastatic tumors
    D. Meningioma

19. Within a neuron, graded potentials

    A. produce graded action potentials
    B. may aggregate in space and time
    C. usually hyperpolarize the membrane
    D. always produce action potentials

20. Diseases of the motor neurons include
    I. Amyotrophic lateral sclerosis
    II. Charcot-Marie-Tooth (CMT) disease
    III. Werndig-Hoffman diseases
    IV. Huntington's Disease

    A. I only   B. I and III   C. II, III and IV   D. IV only

21. A subdural hematoma typically occurs

    A. between the dura and the skull
    B. secondary to a rupture of the bridging veins of the brain
    C. secondary to a fracture of the temporal bone
    D. between the cranium and the scalp

22. At the emergency room, a 7-year-old child is listless, has a temperature of 100.6° F, and presents nuchal rigidity. A lumbar puncture yields slightly cloudy cerebrospinal fluid with elevated protein and decreased glucose. A culture of this fluid will most likely yield

    A. aspergillus fumigatus
    B. cryptococcus neoformans
    C. streptococcus pneumoniae
    D. hemophilus influenzae

23. The brain is divided into upper and lower parts by the _____ section.

    A. horizontal
    B. sagittal
    C. coronal
    D. ipsilateral

24. Which of the following is a drug used exclusively in the treatment of absence seizures?

    A. Diazepam
    B. Ethosuxamide
    C. Phenobarbital
    D. Phenytoin (Dilantin)

25. A 48-year-old man has experienced right-sided headaches for nearly 6 years, and has recently noted some weakness in his left hand. A CAT scan shows a well-defined lateral mass that is compressing the right hemisphere in the frontal-parietal area. Most likely, this mass is a(n)

    A. meningioma
    B. glioblastoma multiform
    C. Schwannoma
    D. astrocytoma

KEY (CORRECT ANSWERS)

1.	D	11.	B
2.	C	12.	C
3.	A	13.	C
4.	A	14.	A
5.	A	15.	C
6.	C	16.	B
7.	A	17.	B
8.	C	18.	A
9.	C	19.	B
10.	C	20.	B

21.	B
22.	D
23.	A
24.	B
25.	A

TEST 3

DIRECTIONS: Each question or incomplete statement is followed by several suggested answers or completions. Select the one the BEST answers the question or completes the statement. *PRINT THE LETTER OF THE CORRECT ANSWER IN THE SPACE AT THE RIGHT.*

1. A person experiencing nausea, vomiting, tinnitus, or hearing loss, accompanied by horizontal or rotary nystagmus, is experiencing _____ vertigo.   1.____

    A. migraine
    B. central
    C. peripheral
    D. vascular insufficiency

2. The forebrain is also known as the   2.____

    A. tela choroidea
    B. prosencephalon
    C. superior colliculus
    D. diencephalon

3. Which of the following disorders is associated with pink Lewy bodies?   3.____

    A. Huntington's disease
    B. Alzheimer's disease
    C. Creutzfeld-Jakov disease
    D. Parkinson's disease

4. Which of the following is the location where sound waves are converted to nerve impulses?   4.____

    A. Vestibular system
    B. Inner ear
    C. Middle ear
    D. Brain stem

5. An 82-year-old woman suffers ischemic injury with cerebral infarction. A few days later, it is most likely that the cerebrum will yield a histo-pathological finding of _____ necrosis.   5.____

    A. liquefactive
    B. fat necrosis
    C. coagulative
    D. gangrenous

6. Which of the following is NOT found in the midbrain?   6.____

    A. Cerebral peduncle
    B. Inferior colliculus
    C. Tegmentum
    D. Tectum

7. The "triad of Wernicke-Korsakoff syndrome" includes each of the following, EXCEPT

   A. ophthalmoplegia B. aphasia
   C. ataxia D. psychosis

8. Wallerian degeneration of a peripheral nerve can
   I. be seen in Guillain-Barre syndrome
   II. can occur when the neuron that controls an axon dies
   III. can be followed by regeneration
   IV. can occur following severe trauma or infarction

   A. I and II
   B. II, III and IV
   C. III and IV
   D. I, II, III and IV

9. The theory that all the neurons in the body are physically connected is the _____ hypothesis.

   A. coalition B. reticular C. connectivity D. associative

10. Approximately two-thirds of people with epilepsy have _____ seizures.

    A. tonic-clonic
    B. generalized absence
    C. status epilepticus
    D. complex partial

11. The brain's _____ lobe is involved in the understanding of visual images and the meaning of written words.

    A. frontal B. parietal C. temporal D. occipital

12. Which of the following is NOT consistent with a stroke involving the right middle cerebral artery?

    A. Spatial disorientation
    B. Left hemiparesis
    C. Aphasia
    D. Hemianopsia

13. Wernicke-Korsakoff syndrome affects the
    I. thalamus
    II. mamillary bodies
    III. amygdala

    A. I only B. I and II C. II only D. I, II and III

14. Epinephrine is a
    A. neuropeptide
    B. neurotransmitter
    C. neuron
    D. neurotoxin

15. The postcentral gyrus is a cerebral structure that serves as a(n) _____ cortex.
    A. visual
    B. olfactory
    C. somatosensory
    D. motor

16. Which of the following is MOST likely to be associated with hypertensive arteriosclerosis?
    A. Epidural hematoma
    B. Subarachnoid hemorrhage
    C. Subdural hematoma
    D. Basal ganglia hemorrhage

17. During a radical mastectomy involving a 69-year-old patient, the anesthesiologist reports a drop in blood pressure. If hypotension lasts longer than 30 minutes, the most likely consequence is
    A. parietal lobe hemorrhagic infarct
    B. anterior pituitary necrosis
    C. lacunar infarcts of basal ganglia
    D. linear parasagittal infarction

18. What is the function of neuroglial cells?
    A. Supporting and protecting neurons
    B. Receiving chemical messages
    C. Regulating sodium/potassium levels
    D. Regenerating damaged nerve cell bodies

19. Symptoms of central vertigo can be described as
    I. more subtle and less intense than peripheral vertigo
    II. insidious in onset
    III. usually difficult for the patient to explain
    IV. occasionally including vertical nystagmus

    A. I only
    B. I and II
    C. III only
    D. I, II, III and IV

20. Common symptoms of brain stem neoplasms include each of the following, EXCEPT
    A. dysphagia
    B. vomiting
    C. tinnitus
    D. ataxia

21. The point at which graded potentials in a neuron reach an action potential is known as the

    A. excitatory postsynaptic potential (EPSP)
    B. inhibitory postsynaptic potential (IPSP)
    C. threshold voltage
    D. refractory period

22. Which of the following is LEAST likely to be associated with neural syphilis?

    A. Hemorrhagic encephalitis
    B. Spinal cord dorsal column atrophy
    C. Endarteritis
    D. Chronic meningitis

23. The risk of stroke for a patient with a history of transient ischemic attacks is about _____ % per year and _____ % after five years.

    A. 5; 25
    B. 10; 33
    C. 20; 20
    D. 33; 66

24. The most common site of a central nervous system lymphoma is

    A. the cerebellum
    B. the pons
    C. the spinal cord
    D. one of the cerebral hemispheres

25. The sympathetic and parasympathetic nervous systems are immediate divisions of the _____ nervous system.

    A. vestibular
    B. autonomic
    C. central
    D. peripheral

KEY (CORRECT ANSWERS)

1.	C	11.	D
2.	B	12.	C
3.	D	13.	B
4.	B	14.	B
5.	A	15.	C
6.	D	16.	D
7.	B	17.	D
8.	B	18.	A
9.	B	19.	D
10.	D	20.	C

21. C
22. A
23. B
24. D
25. B

CENTRAL NERVOUS SYSTEM
EXAMINATION SECTION
TEST 1

DIRECTIONS: Each question or incomplete statement is followed by several suggested answers or completions. Select the one that BEST answers the question or completes the statement. *PRINT THE LETTER OF THE CORRECT ANSWER IN THE SPACE AT THE RIGHT.*

1. The skull is made up of _____ bones, which can be categorized as either cranial or facial bones.

    A. 20   B. 18   C. 29   D. 35

2. The facial bones MOST important in emergency medicine include the

    A. maxilla
    B. mandible
    C. zygomata
    D. all of the above

3. The opening in the base of the skull where the brain stem is continuous with the beginning of the spinal cord is called the foramen

    A. magnum
    B. of monro
    C. rotundum
    D. spinosum

4. The one of the following NOT among the three layers of fibrous covering of the brain (meninges) is the

    A. dura mater
    B. tia mater
    C. arachnoid
    D. pia mater

5. The dura mater is firmly attached to the internal wall of the skull. In certain places, however, it splits into two surfaces and forms venous sinuses. During head injury, those sinuses can be disrupted, allowing the blood to collect beneath the dura.
   This condition is known as _____ hematoma.

    A. subdural
    B. epidural
    C. subarachnoid
    D. all of the above

6. The meningeal arteries are located between the dura and the skull. Disruption of one of these arteries results in bleeding above the dura, forming

    A. subdural hematoma
    B. epidural hematoma
    C. subarachnoid hemorrhage
    D. none of the above

7. The brain is

    A. a very soft and moist organ
    B. richly supplied with blood
    C. contained in the skull cavity
    D. all of the above

8. The cerebellum is located in the _____ part of the brain.

   A. anterior
   B. superior
   C. inferoposterior
   D. anteriolateral

9. The MAIN function of the cerebellum is the control of

   A. posture and equilibrium and the coordination of skills
   B. heart rate
   C. vision
   D. speech

10. The brain stem is located at the _____ of the brain.

    A. anterior part
    B. anteriolateral part
    C. base
    D. none of the above

Questions 11-14.

DIRECTIONS: In Questions 11 through 14, match the numbered region of the brain with its lettered function, listed in Column I. Place the letter of the CORRECT answer in the appropriate space at the right.

COLUMN I

A. Speech center
B. Vision center
C. Respiratory center
D. Concerned with emotion

11. Occipital lobe

12. Temporal lobe

13. Frontal lobe

14. Brain stem

15. The functions of brain stem include

    A. the medulla's control of respiration and heart rate
    B. control of the eye, throat, and facial muscles
    C. the oculomotor nerve's causing the eye to constrict
    D. all of the above

16. All of the following are true regarding the spinal cord EXCEPT:

    A. It is 10 mm in diameter.
    B. If the vertebral body is displaced 5 mm, injury to the cord and paralysis may result.
    C. It controls movement of the eye muscles.
    D. There are segmental neurons that supply local anatomical structures.

17. The _____ mediates the position and vibratory sense.

    A. anterior column
    B. posterior column
    C. corticospinal tract
    D. all of the above

18. Of the following, the mediators of pain and temperature sense include the 18.____

    A. corticospinal tract
    B. posterior column
    C. lateral spinothalmic tract
    D. all of the above

19. Movement is usually controlled by 19.____

    A. the corticospinal tract   B. the lateral spinal tract
    C. all of the above   D. none of the above

20. The chemical mediator of the parasympathetic nervous system is 20.____

    A. norepinephrine   B. epinephrine
    C. acetylcholine   D. all of the above

21. Regarding cerebrospinal fluid, it is TRUE that 21.____

    A. it is a clear and water-like fluid
    B. it serves as a shock absorber and as a source of nourishment for some of the brain cells
    C. leakage of the fluid indicates that the skull has been fractured and the dura mater has been lacerated
    D. all of the above

22. When sympathetic nerves are damaged or interrupted, all of the following conditions may occur EXCEPT 22.____

    A. a sudden increase in blood pressure
    B. arteries no longer constricting in response to changes in posture and core body temperature
    C. dramatic pooling of blood within the suddenly dilated vessels
    D. a fall in blood pressure

Questions 23-25.

DIRECTIONS: In Questions 23 through 25, match the numbered description with the lettered structure of the central nervous system, listed in Column I, which it most accurately describes. Place the letter of the CORRECT answer in the appropriate space at the right.

COLUMN I

    A. Dura mater
    B. Arachnoid mater
    C. Pia mater

23. Middle meningeal layer; a delicate, transparent membrane. 23.____

24. A thin, highly vascular membrane firmly adherent to the surface of the brain. 24.____

25. Outermost layer; a strong, fibrous wrapping. 25.____

KEY (CORRECT ANSWERS)

1.	C	11.	B
2.	D	12.	A
3.	A	13.	D
4.	B	14.	C
5.	A	15.	D
6.	B	16.	C
7.	D	17.	B
8.	C	18.	C
9.	A	19.	A
10.	C	20.	C

21. D
22. A
23. B
24. C
25. A

TEST 2

DIRECTIONS: Each question or incomplete statement is followed by several suggested answers or completions. Select the one that BEST answers the question or completes the statement. *PRINT THE LETTER OF THE CORRECT ANSWER IN THE SPACE AT THE RIGHT.*

1. Signs and symptoms of increased intracranial pressure include

    A. rising blood pressure
    B. slow pulse
    C. rapid or irregular respiration
    D. all of the above

    1.____

2. A 25-year-old male is hit with a baseball bat on the right side of his head during a fight. He loses consciousness for a few minutes; then he regains consciousness, but one hour later he starts getting sleepy with a change of mental status. On examination, his right pupil is fixed and dilated.
   The MOST likely diagnosis is

    A. subdural hematoma   B. epidural hematoma
    C. subarachnoid hemorrhage   D. all of the above

    2.____

Questions 3-5.

DIRECTIONS: Questions 3 through 5 are to be answered on the basis of the following information.

You receive a call for a 30-year-old male who fell from the stairs. When you get to the scene, you find an unconscious patient with multiple lacerations on his head and slightly elevated blood pressure.

3. The best FIRST management is

    A. nasotracheal intubation
    B. epinephrine IV
    C. to try to stop the bleeding
    D. to start an IV lifeline

    3.____

4. The MOST likely initial treatment for increased intracranial pressure would be to maintain a ventilation rate of about _____ breaths per minute.

    A. 10   B. 15
    C. 20   D. none of the above

    4.____

5. Which of the following drugs might the physician order if the patient's condition does NOT improve?

    A. Furosemide   B. Manitol
    C. Diazepam   D. A and B *only*

    5.____

6. If a patient with head trauma develops seizures in a pre-hospital setting, you should notify the physician and then administer

   A. phenytoin
   B. diazepam
   C. phenobarbital
   D. none of the above

7. The single MOST important sign in the evaluation of a head-injured patient is

   A. rising blood pressure
   B. decreasing pulse rate
   C. changing state of consciousness
   D. none of the above

8. The Glascow coma scale assigns a numerical score to the patient's responses in three categories.
   The one of the following categories which does NOT receive a score according to this scale is

   A. eye opening
   B. breathing response
   C. best motor response
   D. verbal response

9. _____ is the MOST likely cause of hypotension in a patient with head injury.

   A. Epidural hematoma
   B. Subdural hematoma
   C. Major hemorrhaging elsewhere in the body
   D. All of the above

10. You should suspect spinal cord injury as a result of

    A. vehicular trauma
    B. a diving accident
    C. crush injuries
    D. all of the above

11. The most efficient and readily available means of temporary stabilization are pairs of hands or knees. The MAIN objective of stabilization is to keep the head and neck in the _____ position.

    A. extension
    B. flexion
    C. neutral
    D. none of the above

12. The maneuver performed to open the airway in a spine-injured patient is

    A. jaw thrust
    B. chin lift
    C. jaw lift
    D. all of the above

13. Which of the following findings, if present in a male, is a characteristic sign of spinal cord injury?

    A. Hypotension
    B. Priapism
    C. Bruises of the back
    D. Tachycardia

14. If a patient with suspected spinal cord injury develops signs of shock, you should

    A. inflate the mast
    B. cover the patient with a blanket
    C. establish IV with ringer lactate solution
    D. all of the above

15. The medication which, if given within 8 hours of injury, may permit some recovery of nerve function is   15.____

    A. epinephrine   B. corticosteroids
    C. norepinephrine   D. none of the above

16. A mild, closed head injury without detectable damage to the brain is called a   16.____

    A. concussion   B. contusion
    C. laceration   D. all of the above

17. A bruised brain caused by the force of a blow to the head great enough to rupture the blood vessels is referred to as a   17.____

    A. laceration   B. contusion
    C. concussion   D. all of the above

18. The signs and symptoms indicative of possible skull fracture include   18.____

    A. blood coming from the ears
    B. clear fluid coming from the ears
    C. loss of balance as the patient attempts to position himself
    D. all of the above

19. Proper pre-hospital treatment for a victim who has clear fluid draining from the ear would be to   19.____

    A. pack the sternal ear canal
    B. apply loose sterile external dressing
    C. remove any impaled object(s)
    D. none of the above

20. The ears are responsible for   20.____

    A. hearing   B. equilibrium
    C. control of eye movement   D. A and B *only*

Questions 21-25.

DIRECTIONS: In Questions 21 through 25, match the numbered function with the lettered correlated term, listed in Column I. Place the letter of the CORRECT answer in the appropriate space at the right.

COLUMN I

21. Diaphragm   A. C_4 21.____
22. Knee flexion   B. $S_2 - S_3$ 22.____
                       C. $L_5 - S_1$
23. Bladder control   D. $C_5 - C_6$ 23.____
                       E. $C_7 - L_8 - T_1$
24. Elbow flexion   24.____
25. Finger movement   25.____

Questions 26-30.

DIRECTIONS: In Questions 26 through 30, match the numbered definition with the lettered term in Column I with which it is MOST closely correlated. Place the letter of the CORRECT answer in the appropriate space at the right.

COLUMN I

A. Decebrate posture
B. Decorticate posture
C. Herniation
D. Reticular activating system
E. Countrecoup

26. Extrusion of part of the brain through the tentorium, or foramen magnum, as a result of increased ICP. 26.___

27. Center in the brain stem that controls the state of wakefulness. 27.___

28. Injury resulting from a blow at another site. 28.___

29. Assumed by a patient with severe brain dysfunction; characterized by extension and internal rotation of the arm and extension of the legs. 29.___

30. Characterized by extension of the legs and flexion of the arm. 30.___

KEY (CORRECT ANSWERS)

1.	D	16.	A
2.	B	17.	B
3.	A	18.	D
4.	C	19.	B
5.	D	20.	D
6.	B	21.	A
7.	C	22.	C
8.	B	23.	B
9.	C	24.	D
10.	D	25.	E
11.	C	26.	C
12.	D	27.	D
13.	B	28.	E
14.	D	29.	A
15.	B	30.	B

CENTRAL NERVOUS SYSTEM

Unit 1. Anatomy and Physiology

    Nerve Cells 1
    Brain 1
    Spinal Cord 3
    Peripheral Nervous System 4
    Autonomic Nervous System 5
    Protective Mechanisms for the Central Nervous System 6

Unit 2. Patient Assessment

    History 7
    Physical Examination 8

Unit 3. Pathophysiology and Management

    Pathophysiology of Head Trauma 12
    Spinal Injury 14
    Coma 16
    Seizure 18
    Stroke 21

Unit 4. Techniques of Management

    Spinal Immobilization 23
    Monitoring Patient Status 24

Glossary 25

CENTRAL NERVOUS SYSTEM
Unit 1. Anatomy and Physiology

The nervous system includes the brain and spinal cord, which combine to form the central nervous system (CNS), autonomic nervous system, and the peripheral nervous system. This chapter discusses the anatomy and physiology of the CNS primarily. Brief discussions of the autonomic and peripheral nervous systems, assessment of the patient with possible neurological injury, the pathophysiology of neurological problems, and management techniques for patients with these problems are included.

Nerve Cells

The nerve cell, or neuron, is the basic unit of all the nervous systems. Each neuron is composed of a cell body, which contains the nucleus of the nerve cell; dendrites, which carry impulses to the cell body; and axons, which carry impulses away from the cell body. Collections of cell bodies appear gray and, therefore, are referred to as "gray matter." Axons are often covered with a white myelin sheath, and areas of the nervous system that contain myelinated axons are called "white matter."

Impulses are transmitted along nerves by a combined chemical and electrical process. It may be helpful to think of the nerves as wires surrounded by myelin insulation. Nerve cells can receive impulses (excitability), conduct them (conductivity), and transmit them to a second cell (transmission). Impulses travel from the dendrites to the cell body and then from the cell body down the axon. When an impulse reaches the end of the axon, it is transmitted to a second cell across a junction, called a synapse. The second cell may be another nerve cell, a muscle cell, or a gland cell.

Unlike excitability and conductivity, which are electrical in nature, transmission of impulses from a nerve cell to another cell is chemical. The chemical released by the axon crosses the synaptic junction to excite the second cell. Some drugs and poisons can block this synaptic transmission and prevent excitation of the second cell, while others can lead to a buildup of the chemical transmitter and excess excitation of the second cell.

Brain

The brain is a complex collection of nerve cells and specialized supporting cells located inside a rigid, hard container (skull). A very soft organ, the brain is richly supplied with blood vessels. These characteristics make the brain uniquely susceptible to injury. Although the skull can protect the brain from external injury because of its rigidity and hardness, these same qualities can, in some cases, cause injury to the brain. In some ways, the brain behaves like a sponge inside a steel case; it cannot expand inside the rigid skull. Therefore, swelling of the brain or accumulation of blood within the skull compresses the brain and causes increased pressure inside the skull. This pressure (increased intracranial pressure) causes changes that interfere with the functioning of the brain. Further, because the skull is hard, the brain and blood vessels on the surface of the brain may be damaged if they strike the skull's inner surface. This condition can occur when the head is struck directly or when it is rapidly accelerated or decelerated. The phenomenon of "seeing stars" when struck on the back of the head is due to the occipital poles of the brain banging against the back of the skull.

The brain is suspended inside the skull by ligaments, the function of which is to prevent undue motion. The ligament in the midline is called the falx cerebri. Another ligament, the tentorium cerebelli, runs across the roof of the posterior fossa.

The brain is divided into three main parts: the cerebrum, cerebellum, and brain stem. The cerebrum is the largest part of the brain, occupying the top and front of the skull; it is divided from the front to the back of the skull into left and right cerebral hemispheres. The cerebral cortex is the gray, outer surface layer of the cerebral hemispheres. This thin layer, 2 to 5 millimeters (mm) thick, contains nerve cell bodies. Each cerebral, hemisphere is further divided into four lobes-frontal, temporal, parietal, and occipital-named according to the overlying skull bones. These lobes are separated from each other by fissures.

Each nerve cell contained in the cerebral cortex (cortical nerve cell) has a specialized function, and groups of these cells that perform related functions are located in different areas of the brain. It is important for the paramedic to know these areas because damage to each area, such as that caused by trauma and stroke, causes specific clinical signs and symptoms. The areas are given functional names but also may be referred to by their anatomic location. Damage to the motor cortex causes weakness or paralysis on the opposite side of the body because many nerve fibers from the cortex are crossed in the brain stem and spinal cord. The right side of the brain controls the left side of the body; the left side of the brain controls the right side of the body. The rest of the frontal lobe is involved in the higher mental processes of judgment, foresight, and perseverance. People with damage to this area often have difficulty making appropriate judgments.

In most people, speech is controlled by a small area of the left temporal lobe. Damage to this area causes a variety of difficulties with speech, ranging from inability to find the correct word to total inability to speak. Hearing is controlled by the auditory cortex, located in the superior temporal lobes. Visual sensation is located in the occipital cortex in the posterior part of the cerebrum. Other types of sensory information (touch, pain, temperature, vibration, and position sense) are received and processed by the sensory area in the parietal lobe.

The crossed relationship between the brain and the body also applies to the transmission of sensory information. For example, the sensation of pain caused by a pin sticking the right hand is perceived by the left side of the brain. Conversely, damage to the left sensory cortex will cause a loss of perception of the right side of the body. Because of its anterior and superior location in the skull, the cerebrum is more subject to injury than are other parts of the CMS.

The cerebellum is the second major area of the brain, located in the back, or inferoposterior, part of the skull. The cerebellum has two hemispheres and a thin covering of gray matter over a core of white matter. Unlike the functions of the cerebrum, however, the functions of the cerebellum are not as well localized to specific areas of the cerebellar cortex. In general, the cerebellum maintains posture and balance and coordinates skilled voluntary muscle movements. Therefore, damage to the cerebellum causes difficulties in balancing and coordination, which are noticed most easily when the injured person tries to walk. Fortunately, because of its location in the back of the skull, the cerebellum rarely is injured except by direct trauma to this area.

The brain stem, located at the base of the brain, is the third major part of the brain. It contains nerve tracts formed by groups of axons that carry impulses to and from the brain and the spinal cord. In addition, these structures contain groups of nerve cell bodies, also called nuclei, that control various body functions. The medulla, the part of the brain stem located just above the spinal cord, has centers critical to the maintenance of vital bodily functions such as respiration, heart rate, and blood pressure. Damage to these centers, or interference with their functioning by certain drugs, causes a variety of cardiorespiratory derangements, from bradycardia to cardiopulmonary arrest.

Other centers in the brain stem control the muscles of the eyes, throat, and face and receive sensory information from these areas. From these centers, or nuclei, nerves run through different bony canals to the structures of the face. Damage to the facial nerve, which can be caused by a skull fracture, will paralyze some of the facial muscles. Similarly, damage to the oculomotor nerve will prevent the pupil on the damaged side of the body from responding to light.

Spinal Cord

The spinal cord is the second major part of the CNS. Like the brain, the spinal cord is protected by a bony structure known as the spine. Each section (vertebra) of the spine contains an anterior bony vertebral body to support the body's weight and a posterior bony ring (neural arch) to protect the spinal cord. The spinal canal formed by the neural arch is 15 mm in diameter; inside the canal, the spinal cord is about 10 mm in diameter. Therefore, if vertebra is displaced only 5 nun in any direction, injury to the spinal cord with subsequent paralysis can result.

The spinal cord has a gray matter core that is surrounded by a layer of white matter. The gray matter contains cell bodies, while the white matter contains ascending and descending axons collected in bundles called nerve tracts. These tracts connect the brain with the rest of the body. Three important tracts are (1) the posterior column that mediates position and vibratory sense, (2) the lateral spinal thoracic tract that mediates pain and temperature sensation, and (3) the cortical spinal tract that controls muscle movement. Damage to these tracts can be determined in the injured patient by testing position sense, pain sensation, and the ability to move the extremities.

The spinal cord can be divided into five main areas: the cervical, thoracic, lumbar, sacral, and coccygeal (tailbone). In each section of the cord, nerve cells control motor function an' sensation for specific anatomic structures. At each level of the cord, bundles of nerve fibers join to form nerve roots that leave the front and back sides of the spinal cord and then join to form peripheral nerves. Nerve roots in different areas have control over specific functions. The inability to move the shoulder, for example, indicates injury to the fifth cervical nerve root (C5). The following list shows other important relationships between the nerve root and the function of various body structures:

- Cervical
-- Shoulder girdle (C5)
-- Elbow flexion (C5, C6)
-- Elbow extension (C6, C8)
-- Wrist movement (C6, C7)

- Thoracic
-- Thoracic region movement and sensation (T4 through T10)

-- Sensation at the nipple level (T4)
-- Sensation at the umbilicus level (T10)

- Lumbar
-- Hip flexion (L2, L3)
-- Hip extension (L4, L5)
-- Knee extension (L3, L4)

- Sacral
-- Knee flexion (L5, S1)
-- Ankle movement (S1, S2)
-- Toe movement (L5, S1, S2)

The skin area supplied by cutaneous (skin) nerves from a single nerve root is called a dermatome. Testing skin sensation in different areas is also a way to assess the integrity of specific nerve roots.

Peripheral Nervous System

The peripheral nervous system is complex because branches from the spinal nerves join together with branches from other spinal cord segments to form large bundles or plexuses. These plexuses divide further to form the peripheral nerves that run to the muscles, skin, and other structures in the extremities. The peripheral nerves can be injured by fractures or lacerations of the extremities, causing local - muscular paralysis and loss of sensation.

Branches of the brachial plexus innervate the upper extremity. Five major nerves branch form the brachial plexus:

- Axillary nerve. The axillary nerve supplies the deltoid muscle and skin of the shoulder.
- Musculocutaneous nerve. The musculocutaneous nerve descends laterally to supply the biceps muscle and ends in a cutaneous sensory nerve in the forearm.
- Radial nerve. The radial nerve branches off to the arm and forearm muscles, to the skin of the posterior arm, and to the posterior forearm. When the radial nerve is damaged, motion of and sensation in the thumb are lost.
- Superficial radial nerve. The superficial radial nerve is a cutaneous nerve that innervates the skin of the lateral posterior forearm and lateral posterior hand.
- Deep radial nerve. The deep radial nerve innervates the skin and the muscles of the ulna in the forearm and the hand. Because the ulnar nerve crosses the outer aspect of the elbow, it can be damaged in injuries to this joint, resulting in sensorimotor loss in the little finger.
- Median nerve. The median nerve innervates muscles of the forearm and hand, the skin of the thumb, the first three fingers, and the radial side of the palm.

The lumbosacral plexus innervates the lower extremity. Its major branches include:

- Femoral nerve. The femoral nerve innervates the anterior thigh muscles, including the quadriceps group. In addition, the femoral nerve gives off cutaneous branches to the skin of the anterior and medial distal thigh and the medial leg and foot.
- Obturator nerve. The obturator nerve innervates muscles of the medial thigh and the skin of the distal medial thigh.

- Sciatic nerve. The sciatic nerve is the largest nerve in the body and is found in the posterior thigh. It innervates the muscles of the calf and the back of the thigh and the skin of the lower calf and the upper surface of the foot.
- Superficial peroneal nerve. The superficial peroneal nerve innervates the lateral leg muscles and the skin on the dorsum of the foot.
- Deep peroneal nerve. The deep peroneal nerve innervates the anterior and lateral leg muscles and the muscles that move the toes.
- Tibial nerve. The tibial nerve innervates the skin and muscles of the posterior leg and the sole of the foot. Damage to the tibial nerve results in "foot drop," the inability to dorsoflex the foot.

Autonomic Nervous System

The autonomic nervous system, or involuntary nervous system, stimulates smooth muscle (found in the blood vessels and bowel), heart muscle, and some endocrine glands. This system maintains the various bodily functions over which the individual has no conscious control, including blood pressure, temperature regulation, sweating, and peristaltic activity of the bowel. In stressful situations, the autonomic nervous system also helps the body produce the appropriate "fight or flight" response, characterized by changes in blood flow and metabolism.

The autonomic nervous system is divided into the parasympathetic nervous system, which controls the vegetative functions mentioned above, and the sympathetic nervous system, which prepares the body for stress. The parasympathetic nerves release acetylcholine when stimulated. This chemical transmitter crosses the synaptic junction (neuromuscular junction) to stimulate the end organ, or muscle. Effects of acetylcholine (cholinergic effects) include salivation, pupillary constriction, slowing of the heart, constriction of bronchial smooth muscle, and increased intestinal motility.

Atropine inhibits the breakdown of acetylcholine at the neuromuscular junction, causing increased cholinergic activity. Clinically, atropine is used to increase the heart rate because of this effect. Some insecticides, notably those of the organophosphate type, block cholinergic activity and can lead to fatal paralysis and cardiac arrest unless their effects are countered by treatment with atropine.

The sympathetic nervous system has more widespread effects than the parasympathetic system. Sympathetic chemical transmitters include norepinephrine, which is released from sympathetic nerve endings, and epinephrine (Adrenalin), which is released from the adrenal gland when it is stimulated by the sympathetic nerves. Sympathetic nervous stimulation increases the heart rate (pulse) and the force of cardiac contraction. In the blood vessels, sympathetic stimulation of specialized receptors (called beta-1 and beta-2 adrenergic receptors) can both increase and decrease the muscular tone of the vessel wall. Stimulation of beta receptors, therefore, influences the blood pressure and the blood flow to different parts of the body.

The sympathetic nerves originate from the thoracic and lumbar segments of the spinal cord; damage to these areas can cause derangement of the sympathetic nervous system. Such damage can lead to heat loss and shock; as vascular tone diminishes, pooling of blood in the extremities occurs.

Protective Mechanisms for the Central Nervous System

The brain and the spinal cord are among those body structures that do not have the ability to regenerate if cells are permanently damaged. While some brain cells can take over the functions of other damaged cells, the amount of function regained cannot be predicted and is usually limited. <u>Any patient with possible neurological injury must be handled very carefully in the emergency treatment situation to prevent additional damage.</u>

Fortunately, there are several protective mechanisms for the structures of the CNS. The skull provides a rigid container for the brain, and the spine protects the spinal cord. Within these bony structures, three layers of tissue, called meninges, provide additional protection. The first of these layers is the dura mater, the thick fibrous outer covering of the brain. It is attached to the skull except at the falx cerebri, which separates the two halves of the cerebrum, and the tentorium cerebelli, which separates the occipital lobe of the cerebrum from the cerebellum. These dural infoldings provide a suspension system for the brain and help prevent excessive motion within the skull. The dura mater also forms the outer covering for the spinal cord.

The second layer of tissue is called the arachnoid membrane. Between the arachnoid membrane and the dura mater is the subdural space in which blood vessels and nerves pass to and from the brain. The next layer is the pia mater, which is closely attached to the surface of the brain *and spinal cord* and dips into every fold of their surfaces. Between the arachnoidea and pia mater is the subarachnoid space, which is filled with cerebrospinal fluid (CSF).

The CSF helps protect the brain and spinal cord, providing a cushion between the two and their adjacent bony structures. Clear and colorless, the CSF circulates through and around the brain and spinal cord before being resorbed. When tears in the dura mater occur, usually after skull fractures, the CSF may leak out through the nose or the ears. <u>Leakage of CSF indicates a critical situation as it signals serious injury to the CNS as well as possible infection (meningitis).</u>

Unit 2. Patient Assessment

It is often difficult to assess patients with CNS problems. Because the mental functioning of these patients is often impaired, they may be unable to give coherent histories or to cooperate in physical examinations. In such cases, the paramedic must obtain information from careful observation. All injuries and illnesses that interfere with brain and spinal cord functions are serious. In many cases, improper management of these conditions can cause permanent disability or death. Therefore, careful assessment is particularly important in patients with CNS problems.

History

If Emergency Medical Technician-Paramedics (EMT-P's) cannot obtain a history from a patient, they can question bystanders or family members, as well as observe the environment in which the patient is found. If the patient is a trauma victim, answers to the following questions are particularly important:

- When did the accident occur?
- How did it occur? What were the mechanisms of injury? Did the patient sustain a direct blow to a specific part of the head or spine? Was the spine flexed, extended, or twisted? Was there a rapid deceleration?
- Was the patient unconscious at any time? For how long?
- If the patient is able to communicate, what is the chief complaint? Does the patient experience any pain, numbness, tingling, or paralysis? Have the symptoms changed since the accident?
- Are there possible complicating factors such as significant underlying medical problems or recent ingestion of drugs or alcohol?
- Has the patient moved or been moved since the accident?

The history of the patient with nontraumatic CNS problems also is important, and, if sufficient history can be obtained, an understanding of the patient's problem should he possible in more than 80 percent of cases. The paramedic should try to determine:

- The chief complaint and the details of the present illness, if the patient can communicate.
- Whether the patient has any underlying medical problems

    - Does the patient have heart trouble (cardiac arrhythmias), which may lead to syncopal episodes?
    - Is the patient a chronic seizure patient who has not taken prescribed medications?
    - Is the patient a diabetic who took too much or too little insulin?
    - Does the patient have hypertension?
    - Has the patient ever had symptoms like these before?

- Whether there are any environmental clues that could provide important information if the patient cannot communicate

    - Are there any medicine bottles in the patient's pockets, in a purse, or around the home, for example?
    - Does the patient wear a Medic-Alert tag or carry a card indicating epilepsy or diabetes?
    - Are there any alcohol bottles or drug paraphernalia in the vicinity?

Physical Examination

The physical examination begins with the primary survey. The EMT-P should check the patient's pulse and screen the patient for any life-threatening problems. Such problems should be identified and treated before the patient is given a detailed neurological examination. If the patient is unconscious, special attention must be applied to maintaining an open airway. All trauma victims must be assumed to have cervical spine injuries until proven otherwise; therefore, the paramedic should not hyperextend the patient's neck to open the airway. The "chin lift" or the "jaw thrust" is usually an effective maneuver allowing placement of an oropharyngeal or nasopharyngeal. airway in the unconscious patient.

Patients with major head trauma and serious neurological injury frequently suffer respiratory arrest. Increased intracranial pressure, caused by bleeding within the skull, can exert pressure on vital control centers and can decrease the patient's ability to breathe. Direct injury to the medullary breathing centers also can lead to decreased or absent respirations. If there are facial injuries, blood can flow into the airway and be aspirated into the lungs. If an unconscious patient vomits, stomach contents, including swallowed blood, also can be aspirated. The protection usually given by the gag reflex is absent in these patients. In many patients, airway blockage also can occur simply because the tongue flops back and obstructs the throat. The chin lift or jaw thrust easily solves this type of airway obstruction.

After an airway is assured, the vital signs should be checked carefully. Patients with neurological injury may have changing vital signs, and because the pattern of these changes can aid the EMT-P in making management decisions, the vital signs should be rechecked frequently.

The pattern of respiration and the respiratory rate may vary with the nature and extent of the brain injury. The breathing pattern may be normal, or the patient may exhibit Cheyne-Stokes respiration. In this situation, respirations increase in rate and depth until the patient is hyperventilating and then decrease until the patient appears apneic. Additionally, the patient may exhibit central neurogenic hyperventilation, which is a sustained pattern of deep and rapid breathing. Following central neurogenic hyperventilation, the patient may exhibit ataxic respiration, in which breathing becomes irregular and ineffective. The patient eventually may stop breathing following a period of ataxic respiration. Since many patients with serious neurological injury follow this sequence of breathing patterns, serial observations are important for good patient management.

Cervical spinal cord injuries also can impair respiration. "High" cervical cord damage (at C3) can produce complete respiratory muscle paralysis. Damage at the C5 to C6 level will paralyze the diaphragm, but intercostal muscles will continue to function. Paramedics must remember that neck injuries must be treated very carefully to prevent further damage.

Characteristic changes in blood pressure also occur as intracranial pressure rises. During the early stages of increasing intracranial pressure, the pulse slows while the blood pressure and temperature rise. Later, as the pulse rate increases, the blood pressure falls to normal or hypotensive levels while the temperature remains elevated. These changes develop over time, thus emphasizing the necessity for paramedics to make serial observations of the patient's vital signs. If the patient has low blood pressure and a rapid pulse initially, he or she may be suffering from hemorrhagic, cardiogenic, or neurogenic shock. The paramedic should look for other injuries-for example, a fractured femur or a ruptured abdominal organ-before explaining changes in vital signs on the basis of neurological injury alone.

After checking and recording the vital signs, the paramedic should conduct a head-to-toe survey, paying particular attention to skull injuries. Skull injuries may be closed or open. Asgalp laceration may bleed profusely; however, a patient with a skull fracture may not have obvious signs of such an injury on initial inspection. Therefore, the paramedic should palpate the skull carefully, looking for asymmetry or depression of the skull bones. Blood coming from the ears may also indicate a skull fracture. Blood coming from the nose most often flows from a nasal injury, but it, too, can indicate a skull fracture. Clear fluid coming from the ears or nose is CSF, indicating a major skull fracture with a tear of the dura mater. Ecchymosis behind the ear and over the mastoid bone is called Battle's sign and indicates a basilar skull fracture. Ecchymosis around the eyes (raccoon sign) also suggests a basilar skull fracture.

Following the head-to-toe survey, the paramedic should assess the patient's higher neurological function by checking his or her state of consciousness. Descriptive words like "stupor" or "semicoma" should be avoided when describing the patient's condition because each paramedic, nurse, or doctor will interpret these words differently. Behavioral terms should be used instead; that is, the paramedic should describe what the patient can and cannot do. To assess whether the patient is alert and oriented to person, place, time, and situation, the paramedic can ask the patient for his or her name; the day of the week, date, and year; where he or she is; and where he or she lives. A patient also can be asked what is happening and why the ambulance was called. In addition to assessing the level of consciousness, this questioning process aids in gathering information about the patient. The patient's rate of speech also should be noted. Is the patient's speech rambling, garbled (unintelligible), or absent? Does the patient respond appropriately to questions? Does the patient respond rapidly or sluggishly to commands? Does the patient make purposeful or uncoordinated movements?

If patients are not alert, do they awaken when their name is called, when shaken, or when painful stimuli are applied to varying degrees? The standard painful stimulus is a knuckle pressed forcefully into the patient's sternum with varying degrees of pressure or a pin stuck into the skin of the arm or leg. The patient's reaction to painful stimuli is an important indicator of mental functioning. If the patient attempts to push the paramedic's arm away, movements are purposeful. In major neurological injury, the patient may respond to painful stimuli with stereotyped postures. In decerebrate posturing, the arms and legs are both extended; in decorticate posturing, the arms are flexed but the legs remain extended.

Next, the patient's pupils should be checked, and pupil size of each eye should be compared one with the other; (Some people have slightly unequal pupils normally; thus, this sign is less significant if the patient is conscious.) Are the pupils abnormally dilated or constricted? Heroin causes very small pupils; many other drugs cause large pupils. Do the pupils react quickly to light directly (when the light is shined into the eye being tested) and consensually (when the light is shined into the other eye)? In cases of increased intracranial pressure, compression of the nerve controlling pupil constriction leads to dilation of the pupil, that is, a "blown pupil". When checking the patient's pupils, the paramedic also should remove contact lenses if present.

The extraocular eye movements are also important when examining patients' eyes. Inability to move the eyes appropriately indicates damage to the nerves leading to the eyes or to the brain stem nuclei controlling these nerves. If patients are conscious, they should be asked to follow the paramedic's fingers or a light to the extreme left, then up and down, then to the extreme right, and up and down. The eyes should move fully, in a coordinated fashion. Minor abnormalities of eye motion may be missed unless the patient is asked to look all the way to the left, the right, and up and down.

If the patient is unconscious, the paramedic can check the integrity of these neurological pathways by performing the "doll's eye" maneuver. If the possibility of cervical spine injury has been ruled out, the patient's head should be rotated quickly from side to side while the eyes are held open. The eyes should lag behind the motion of the head, as in some toy dolls; if the eyes move with the head, serious brain damage is present. A checklist has been developed by the American College of Surgeons* to help paramedics and physicians record this information accurately. The rescue vehicle should be equipped with a supply of these forms, and they should be used in the assessment of patients with neurological damage.

After examining the head and assessing the higher mental functions, the patient should be checked for spinal injury. If there is any question of serious spinal damage the patient should be immobilized first and assessed later. If the patient's back can be seen, the paramedic should look for cuts and bruises near or over the spine and note whether there is any obvious deformity of the spine. Paramedics should run their fingers down the spine, feeling for any bony protrusions and noting any painful areas. Finally, the patient should be checked for any visible paralysis of the extremities. If bony deformity or obvious paralysis is present, the patient should be immobilized first, and the assessment continued as appropriate.

Because loss of function occurs below an injured segment of the spinal cord, the survey should be started at the lowest point of the lower extremities, the feet. Motion, sensation, and proprioception (position sense) should be checked. The communicative patient can be asked if he or she can feel the feet and legs being touched. The patient should also be asked if he or she can wiggle the toes or raise the legs. The paramedic can move the patient's toes up and down without the patient seeing and ask the patient to tell in which direction the toes are being moved. The toes should be held on either side rather than on the top and bottom, to avoid giving the patient misleading clues. If the patient can perform these simple tests without difficulty, the integrity of the posterior column, lateral spinal thoracic tract, and cortical spinal tract has been demonstrated, and there is no indication of damage to the spinal cord. If the patient can perform these tests but only to a limited degree with pain, there may be pressure on, or damage to, the cord. The patient should be immobilized in this case. If the patient cannot perform any of these tests, there is a strong indication of severe damage to the spinal cord. This patient also should be immobilized to prevent any further damage to the cord.

The function of the upper extremities (arms), which can be impaired by damage to the spinal cord in the neck (cervical spine), should be checked. The same basic procedures used to assess the function of the lower extremities are followed when testing the upper extremities. The paramedic should touch the patient's hands and arms and ask whether the touch can be felt. The patient's finger can be moved up and down to determine if he or she knows in which direction it is being moved. The patient should be asked to squeeze the paramedic's fingers tightly. The average adult should be able to squeeze tightly enough so that it will be difficult for the paramedic to remove his or her fingers. If the patient can perform all of these tests, there is no indication of cervical cord damage. If the patient has difficulty, damage to the cord is likely. If a cooperative patient is unable to perform any of these tests, the damage is confirmed in the neck. The neck, therefore, should be immobilized. The EMT-P should attempt to confirm the level of the injury by performing a dermatome survey; that is, checking where the patient loses sensation. The paramedic should remember that patients who cannot communicate verbally may be able to respond to commands.

*For a copy, write to the attention of the Trauma Department, American College of Surgeons, 55 East Erie Ave., Chicago, Ill. 60611.

If certain patients are unable to respond to commands, as a result of loss of consciousness, for example, the paramedic can assess neurological damage by jabbing the patient lightly on the sole of the foot or the ankle with a sharp object. If the spinal cord is intact, reflexes will cause the foot to pull back in response. If there is no response, there may be paralysis or the patient may be deeply comatose. This test should be repeated on both feet and both hands.

When checking for paralysis, the paramedic should test all extremities, both right and left. Paralysis in both legs (paraplegia) or in both arms and both legs (quadriplegia) indicates spinal cord damage. Paralysis of the arm and leg on one side of the body (hemiplegia) may indicate a stroke or cerebrovascular accident (CVA). The most reliable sign of spinal cord damage is paralysis, but this sign may not be present despite cord damage. Spinal cord damage can coexist with deformities of the spine and pain, tenderness, cuts, or bruises in the spinal area. If there is any question of spinal cord damage, the patient should be immobilized. While performing the complete neurological assessment, the paramedic should continue to monitor vital signs, level of consciousness, and pupillary reflexes. Patients should be carefully watched for the development of shock.

In summary, assessment of the patient with possible neurological injury involves appropriate history and physical examination. The presence or absence of trauma must be ascertained. Paramedics should find answers to the following questions: What happened? How long ago? Are there any complicating factors? Is there any pain, numbness, or loss of motion or sensation? The patient's head should he checked in an attempt to determine the presence of skull injuries and to assess the level, of consciousness and the presence or absence of pupillary signs. The spine should be checked next for deformity, pain, or tenderness. Paramedics then should test patients for signs of paralysis, first checking the legs and the arms. Vital signs should be assessed frequently, as should the state of consciousness and the state of the pupils; paramedics should be alert to changes that indicate a deterioration of the patient's condition.

Unit 3. Pathophysiology and Management

Pathophysiology of Head Trauma

Head trauma can injure the scalp, the skull, or the brain. The scalp bleeds easily when injured, but the brain usually is not injured in superficial scalp lacerations. If the skull is fractured, however, at least minimal brain injury must be suspected. The brain can be injured either directly or indirectly, and it may be injured without apparent scalp or skull damage.

The protective mechanisms of the brain have already been discussed. When the brain is forced to move rapidly within the skull (e.g., when a victim is hit on the head), the areas in the brain stem that control consciousness become damaged, resulting in the victim losing consciousness. If the injury is minor, the patient will regain consciousness rapidly. The longer the period of unconsciousness, the more severe the damage to the brain. This syndrome is called concussion. A more severe injury produces tissue damage in the brain stem and is called brain stem contusion. The surface of the cerebral hemispheres (cerebral cortex) may be damaged directly if it strikes the inner surface of the skull; this situation produces cerebral contusion. Such injury may produce memory loss, confusion, or other signs, but it usually does not produce unconsciousness by itself. Patients with direct brain injury-brain stem concussion, brain stem contusion, and cerebral contusion-usually remain stable or improve over time.

In contrast, patients with indirect brain injury caused by blood accumulating within the skull usually deteriorate over time. Accumulation of blood within the skull results in increased intracranial pressure, thus compressing vital structures of the brain and brain stem. An epidural hematoma occurs when the middle meningeal artery, located between the skull and the dura mater, is torn by a skull fracture. Blood can collect rapidly. With such an injury, the patient is often unconscious from a brain stem concussion, then regains consciousness, but begins to deteriorate as blood collects in the skull resulting in increased intracranial pressure. In a subdural hematoma, bleeding is from torn veins between the dura mater and the arachnoid mater. The subdural hematoma usually develops more slowly than the epidural hematoma, and deterioration occurs more gradually. When the blood clot is large enough, intracranial pressure increases, and respiratory and other centers are compressed. Often the nerve controlling the pupillary constrictor muscle is compressed causing the pupil to dilate widely, a sign indicative of severe brain damage. Eventually, the cardiorespiratory centers stop functioning, and the patients with indirect brain injury will stop breathing. Because these patients deteriorate over time as the collection of blood inside the skull increases in size, serial observations must be made in assessing the patient with neurological injury. Neurosurgical intervention with drainage of the intracranial hematoma can be life saving in these patients.

In extremely severe head injuries, the skull may be broken and pieces of bone driven into the brain matter. Destruction of cortical cells occurs. If the patient survives, neurological functions will be lost depending on the quantity and location of the cortical cells lost or damaged. If the skull is broken in such a way that the brain is exposed, significant damage to brain tissue usually will occur very quickly. These patients are susceptible to serious infections of the brain (cerebritis) and meninges (meningitis).

It is important that paramedics remember that head injury almost never causes shock, except in infants and small children. Therefore, if an older patient with a head injury is in shock, the paramedic should look elsewhere to find the cause.

Head trauma is commonly sustained as a result of auto accidents, falls, and direct blows to the head. The most important part of the assessment is determining whether the patient's neurological function is changing and, if so, how. Repeated neurological examinations will have to be performed, both in the field and in transit, and an accurate record of these examinations will have to be kept. Patients who show signs of improvement may simply need to he observed in the emergency room or in the hospital, but those patients who show rapid deterioration may require urgent neurosurgical intervention.

An accurate history can he of great value in determining the potential seriousness of the injury. Paramedics should obtain the following information from the patient with head trauma:

- What was the mechanism of injury?
- Did the patient lose consciousness? When? How long was the patient unconscious? Did unconsciousness occur immediately after the accident, or later?
- Did the patient vomit? Children frequently vomit after head injury, but vomiting in adults after head injury may indicate serious intracranial problems.
- What symptoms does the patient have now? Headache? Dizziness? Double vision or blurred vision? Nausea? Weakness? Can the patient move all extremities? Does the patient have any pain in the head, neck, or spine? Does the patient have numbness or a "pins-and-needles" sensation?
- Has the patient ingested any alcohol or drugs in the past few hours?

The physical examination must be performed after the history is taken, and it should be repeated several times. The primary survey should be conducted first. A patient should not be moved until it has been determined that there is no associated spinal injury. <u>A patient with significant head trauma always is assumed to have a cervical spine injury until proven</u> otherwise. Paramedics should handle patients accordingly. The airway should be kept clear, and the paramedic should be satisfied that the patient is breathing adequately. The patient's pulse should be checked. Active bleeding should be halted by direct pressure. The paramedic then should observe other parts of the body for life-threatening injuries, such as sucking chest wounds or severe lacerations.

The vital signs should be taken and repeated at 5-minute intervals. The rate and pattern of the respirations should be noted. The paramedic should determine whether an abnormal pattern is present or whether the patient is breathing only with his or her diaphragm. Any changes n blood pressure over time should be noted also.

The blood pressure may rise as intracranial pressure increases. Falling blood pressure is rarely caused by head injury; if it accompanies head injury, the paramedic must look for a source of major hemorrhage elsewhere in the body. For example, pelvic or femoral fractures are not uncommon in automobile accident victims arid are associated with significant hidden blood loss. EMT-P's should determine whether the pulse increases or decreases. A slow pulse usually accompanies a rise in blood pressure in patients with increasing intracranial pressure. However, a rising pulse also may signal impending shock from bleeding somewhere else in the body.

The head should be examined carefully. Are there scalp lacerations or depressions in the skull? Is there blood or clear fluid in the ear canals? Are there ecchymoses behind the ears (Battle's sign) or around the eyes (raccoon sign)? Is clear fluid leaking from the nose? If clear fluid, presumed to be CSF, is leaking from the ears or the nose, the EMT-P should not attempt to block the flow but should simply cover the ear or nose with sterile gauze.

The patient's neck should be assessed next. Manual traction should be maintained while the paramedic palpates the patient's neck for vertebral irregularities or tenderness. The conscious patient can tell the paramedic whether his or her neck hurts. The comatose or confused patient, on the other hand, will not he able to tell the paramedic what hurts. When in doubt, the EMT-P should maintain traction and apply a cervical collar or immobilize the neck by other methods.

The standard physical exam should he completed in usual head-to-toe order, and the paramedic should look for fractures or lacerations. The patient should never be moved until the whole length of the spinal column is checked.

A neurological exam should then be conducted, and the findings should be recorded carefully. Is the patient alert? Is the patient oriented? Is the patient able to understand questions and to obey simple commands? What type of stimuli are required to make the patient respond if the patient is not fully alert? Can the patient make purposeful movements? The EMT-P should describe what the patient can and cannot do in behavioral rather than descriptive terms, as these often have different meanings for different medical personnel. The eye movements should be checked, and in an unconscious patient the "doll's eyes" response should be looked for. The pupils' reactions to light also should be assessed.

In the field, there is relatively little specific treatment for the patient with head injury. The cardinal principles are to maintain the patient's current status and to prevent further injury. The EMT-P can accomplish these ends by taking the following steps:

- Keep the patient in a supine position.
- Establish an airway, being careful not to aggravate possible cervical spine injury.
- Maintain axial traction on the neck, and apply a cervical collar whenever associated cervical injury is a possibility.
- Administer oxygen, and assist ventilations if necessary.
- Start an intravenous (IV) line with 5 percent dextrose in water (D5W) at a keep open rate. Be careful not to infuse too much fluid-too much fluid can increase the cerebral edema that may occur in head injury.
- Monitor cardiac rhythm, which may be altered if the brain stem is damaged.
- Alert the receiving facility of the patient's condition and estimated time of arrival so that a neurosurgical team can be notified if necessary.
- Transport the patient smoothly, in a supine position if possible. Remember to continue taking vital signs and to check the neurological status en route, recording the results of each examination.

<u>Spinal Injury</u>

Like the brain, the spinal cord can be damaged by direct injury. The spine, however, has less protection than the brain because its bony protection is flexible. The thoracic vertebrae are splinted by the ribs and associated muscles, so injury to the thoracic spine is relatively rare. The neck, however, lacks this support and is the most flexible part of the spine; thus, injuries to the cervical cord are quite common. The size and muscular protection of the lumbar spine make it somewhat more resistant to injury than the cervical spine, but less resistant than the thoracic spine.

The cord is injured by compression from flexion or twisting, laceration or compression from bony fragments of the spine in spinal fractures, protrusion of the cartilage disks between vertebrae into the spinal canal, dislocation of one vertebra from the vertebra below it, or bleeding into the spinal canal, which can result in a spinal epidural hematoma or cause the cord to compress. All suspected injuries should be treated as actual spinal cord injuries to avoid further damage to the cord.

When the spinal cord is lacerated or compressed, nerve fibers that carry impulses (messages) to and from the brain are disrupted. There is a direct relationship between the location of a spinal cord injury and any loss of function in the extremities. This relationship is based on the distribution of nerves that branch off the spinal cord at each segmented level. When a specific pathway is interrupted, the function of the extremity served by that nerve will be affected. In other words, when the pathway is broken, the message cannot be carried.

The initial care of the patient with spinal injury can determine whether he or she regains normal function or is permanently crippled. In few other areas of emergency care will the paramedic's care be so critical to the patient's future. To avoid further injury to the patient, the paramedic must be knowledgeable and skilled in the management of spinal trauma. Again, the history can provide important clues to the nature of the injury, and to its subsequent management. Spinal injury should be suspected in patients injured in automobile, sledding, or diving accidents, as well as falls. The paramedic should try to determine the precise circumstances of the accident. Was the neck flexed, extended, or twisted? When did the accident occur? (If more than 6 hours have elapsed since the accident occurred, the chance of restoring any lost function is greatly diminished.) Does the patient have localized pain in the neck or back? Is there numbness or tingling in any extremity? Are the extremities weak? If the patient is unable to move, the paramedic should find out if the patient was able to move at any time after the accident. A patient who has any movement at all after spinal injury has a better chance of recovering nerve function. It is, therefore, important for the physician to identify these patients. Has the patient been moved since the accident? Have symptoms changed since the injury?

The physical examination of the patient with possible spinal injury is similar to that described for patients with head injury. During the primary survey, initial examination, and examination for vital signs, the patient should he moved as little as possible. The patient should be log rolled while the paramedic maintains axial traction on the head such that the back can be inspected for swelling or hematoma of the spine. This symptom usually indicates vertebral fracture. Any deformities or local tenderness in this area also should he palpated. Paravertebral muscle spasm, encountered during the examination, is a protective mechanism and also can indicate an injured area of the spine. Any open injuries of the spinal column should be covered immediately with sterile dressings. A dermatome survey should be performed with a pin or other sharp object to check for any loss of sensation or motion. Paramedics should he familiar with the innervation points of various spinal nerves. Thus, if sensation is present at the nipples (T4) but absent at the umbilicus MO), the injury is probably between the 5th and 10th thoracic vertebra. The paramedic should check position sense, pain sensation, and movement in the extremities, determining the answers to the following questions:

Can the patient move all extremities? Is strength equal bilaterally? Is the patient unable to perform any specific movements? Spinal injury can damage the sympathetic nervous system and cause blood pressure to fall precipitously. The patient also may be unable to conserve body heat and should not be left uncovered for prolonged periods.

As with head injury, management is aimed at supporting vital functions and preventing further spinal cord damage. To manage spinal injuries, the EMT-P should

- Establish and maintain an airway, being careful not to worsen possible cervical spine injury.
- Administer oxygen and assist ventilation as needed.
- Maintain axial traction and immobilize the neck with a cervical collar. Sandbags can help limit neck motion.
- Immobilize the patient on a long spine board whenever a spinal injury may have occurred. <u>When in doubt immobilize.</u> Patients will not be harmed by unnecessary spinal immobilization, but they can be seriously injured if they do have spinal injuries and are not immobilized.
- Start an IV with D5W. Treat shock if it is present.
- Keep the patient covered to avoid heat loss.
- Notify the receiving facility of the patient's condition and the estimated time of arrival. Patients with spinal injury should be transported to a fully staffed and equipped spinal cord trauma center if possible. Be familiar with the facilities in the community.

Paramedics should remember that damage to the spine does not produce neurological defects unless damage to the spinal cord has also occurred. Every spine injury, especially above the clavicles, should be treated as if a fracture exists. In treating spinal injury, paramedics should never underestimate the possible damage or its consequences.

Coma

Coma may be defined as an abnormally deep state of unconsciousness from which patients cannot be aroused by external stimuli. Coma can be caused by illness or injury. A normal level of consciousness requires continuous interaction between the cerebral hemispheres and various structures in the brain stem. Varying degrees of unconsciousness can occur from depression or destruction of either of these two components. Factors causing coma include direct damage to the brain stem, as in a concussion; an expanding lesion within the skull, such as an intracranial hematoma, which causes pressure on the brain stem; or metabolic states that depress neurologic function widely. Very often it will he difficult to determine the cause of coma and to treat it in the field. Thus, the paramedic's role will, be to maintain the patient until transfer to a medical care facility can be accomplished.

Since the comatose patient obviously cannot give a history, the paramedic must rely on bystanders, family members, and observations of the environment. The EMT-P should seek answers to the following questions: How long has the patient been comatose? Did this state begin suddenly, or did the patient lapse into coma gradually? Did the patient suffer a blow to the head recently, or in the last few weeks? Is the patient under a doctor's care for any conditions? Is the patient known to be a drug or alcohol abuser? Did the patient complain of any symptoms before becoming comatose?

The EMT-P should check bureau tops, medicine cabinets, kitchen counters, refrigerators, and the patient's pockets for medications that might give a clue to any underlying illness. The paramedic also should look for evidence that the patient may be diabetic or epileptic by checking for a Medic Alert bracelet or necklace or a card in the wallet or purse. The area in which the patient is found should he checked for indications of alcohol or drug abuse as well; check for liquor bottles or drug paraphernalia. Paramedics must remember common causes of coma, which are described below, and try to obtain information that will help narrow the possibilities.

- Trauma may not be apparent from a cursory examination of the patient. A complete neurological examination should be performed on the comatose patient.

- The patient may be in a coma from either hypoglycemia (low blood sugar) or insulin reaction (ketoacidosis). To determine whether the patient is diabetic, the paramedic should seek answers to the following questions
  -- Does the patient wear a Medic Alert bracelet?
  -- Is the patient carrying any medication? (Diabinese and Orinase are two medicines frequently taken by adult diabetics.)
  -- Are there insulin syringes in the house, or is there insulin in the refrigerator?
  -- Does the patient's breath have a fruity odor?

- There are rarer causes of coma than diabetes, and it is important for paramedics; to know them. Again, the Medic Alert tag should be looked for as it can indicate thyroid, adrenal, renal, or other problems. The surroundings should be checked for any medications that indicate other serious medical problems.

- Drug overdose is a common cause of coma. Paramedics should attempt to find answers to the following questions

  -- Are there needle tracks on the arms?
  -- Are the pupils pinpoint in size (suggesting heroin overdose) or widely dilated (suggesting barbiturate overdose)?
  -- Is the patient carrying any sedative drugs?
  -- Are there any notes nearby left by the patient?
  -- Are the respirations very slow and deep?

- Paramedics should ask the following questions when stroke or other hypertensive emergencies are suspected

  -- What is the blood pressure?
  -- Are the pupils equal and reactive?
  -- Is one side of the body paralyzed?
  -- Is the patient carrying any antihypertensive medication?

- To determine the possibility of meningitis, the following questions should he answered

  -- Did the patient have severe headaches before the coma began?
  -- Did the patient have a fever or behave in a confused manner?
  -- Does the patient have a rash?
  -- Is the neck rigid?

- In cases of seizures, EMT-P's should seek answers to the following questions

    -- Does the patient have a history of seizures?
    -- Were there witnesses to the patient's seizure?
    -- Is the patient carrying medicines for seizures? Three common medications are Dilantin, phenobarbital, and Mysoline.

- To determine the possibility of alcoholic coma, the following questions should be answered

    -- Is there a smell of alcohol on the patient's breath?
    -- Are there alcohol bottles lying around?

    A patient who has alcohol on the breath, or who is a known alcoholic, may be comatose from other causes. The patient must be checked carefully.

With the exception of trauma and stroke, the common causes of coma can be remembered by the mnemonic AEIOU: Acidosis-diabetes and other types of acidoses; Epilepsy; Infection-meningitis; Overdose-alcohol and drugs; Uremia-kidney failure and other metabolic disorders.

Because the patient cannot tell the paramedic what hurts and because little or no history may be obtainable, the physical examination must be especially thorough. A complete neurological evaluation should be performed as outlined in earlier parts of this chapter.

The cardinal principle of the management of comatose patients is to remember that they have lost the ability to protect themselves and are dependent on their rescuers entirely. To manage the comatose patient effectively, the paramedic should:

- Establish and maintain an airway. The comatose patient has often lost reflexes that prevent aspiration. Insert an oropharyngeal airway and determine whether the patient gags. If this happens, the patient has sufficient reflex activity left and can he managed without intubation. If not, the patient is in danger of aspirating and should be intuhated if there is any question of the airway status.
- Support ventilation as necessary. Administer low-flow oxygen.
- Start an IV with D5W to keep the vein open, simultaneously drawing blood for laboratory studies.
- Obtain orders to administer 25 grams (g) of glucose IV.
- If the pupils are pinpoint, if needle tracks are present on the patient's arms, or if there are other suggestions of drug abuse, consult the physician about administering the narcotic antagonist naloxone (Narcan). Administer Narcan with a slow IV, and observe the patient for an improvement in respiration or level of consciousness. Narcan is short acting and may have to be given repeatedly.
- Monitor the patient by telemetry or a portable unit.
- Transport the patient to the hospital in a supine position while watching respiration.

Seizure

Seizures result from the massive electrical discharge of one or more groups of neurons in the brain, variety of medical conditions increase the instability or irritability of the brain and can lead to seizures; these include stroke, lead trauma (recent or in the past), withdrawal from drugs or alcohol, hypoxia, hypoglycemia, and meningitis. Most patients with seizures have idiopathic epilepsy; that is, the cause of the seizures is not known.

There are four main types of seizures:

- Generalized motor seizures (grand mal seizures), which are characterized by loss of consciousness, tonic clonic movements (characterized by phases of muscle contraction as well as phases of alternating muscle contraction and relaxation) and sometimes tongue biting, incontinence, and mental confusion. The grand mal seizure is often frightening to witness and is the type of seizure for which emergency assistance will most often be summoned. The Latin word for seizure is ictus; the seizure itself is usually followed by a period of coma or drowsiness, the postictal state.
- Focal motor seizures, which usually cause one part of the body (e.g., one side of the face or an arm) to twitch. Focal seizures can progress to generalized seizures. If the seizure is witnessed, note where the twitching started and in which direction the eyes deviated; this information may help the physician to localize the irritable focus in the brain.
- Psychomotor seizures (temporal lobe seizures), which are characterized by an altered personality state often preceded by dizziness or a peculiar metallic taste in the mouth. In some patients, temporal lobe seizures may cause sudden, unexplained attacks of rage; in others, these seizures are manifested by automatic types of behavior.
- Petit mal seizures, which usually occur in children and are rarely an emergency. They are characterized by a brief loss of consciousness without loss of motor tone. The child suddenly stares off into space for a few seconds and then returns immediately to consciousness without any motor symptoms.

These four types of seizures, which represent temporary cerebral dysfunction, must be distinguished from hysterical seizures that represent psychological disorders. Hysterical seizures almost invariably occur in front of an audience. The movements are bizarre and often can be interrupted by a sharp command; the patients rarely injure themselves, bite their tongues, or are incontinent. With experience, usually it is not difficult for the paramedic to distinguish the hysterical from the genuine seizure.

Because of the nature of the electrical discharge in the brain, seizures usually follow a typical sequence. Many patients experience an aura, a peculiar sensation lasting a few seconds that precedes and warns of an impending epileptic attack. The aura may consist of auditory or visual hallucinations, a peculiar taste in the mouth, or a painful sensation in the abdomen. The patient then loses consciousness and enters the tonic phase of continuous motor tension, followed by a hypertonic phase with extreme muscular rigidity and hyperextension of the back. During the clonic phase, rigidity alternates with relaxation, and the patient may be incontinent. There is a massive autonomic discharge, accompanied by hyperventilation, salivation, and tachycardia. Finally, the patient falls into a postictal stupor, from which he or she awakes confused and with a headache. Knowledge of this sequence can help distinguish the grand mal from the hysterical seizure.

The following points are important when obtaining the history from the seizure patient, the family, or bystanders:

- Does the patient have a history of seizures? How frequently do they usually occur? Does the patient take medication for seizures? Has the patient been taking medicines according to the doctor's instructions?
- What did the seizure look like? How long did the seizure last? It may be necessary to obtain this information from bystanders if the paramedic has not witnessed the seizure. Was the seizure preceded by an aura? Did it begin in one area of the body and progress to others? In which direction did the patient's eyes deviate? Did the patient bite his or her tongue or become incontinent?
- Does the patient have a recent or remote history of head trauma? Trauma can cause irritable foci in the brain that can cause seizures.
- Does the patient abuse alcohol or drugs? If so, when was the last time alcohol or drugs were used? Seizures often occur during withdrawal from alcohol and barbiturates.
- Has the patient had a recent fever, headache, or stiff neck? These signs could indicate meningitis.
- Is there any history of diabetes (hypoglycemia can cause seizures), heart disease (arrhythmias can cause cerebral hypoxia that can lead to seizures), or stroke (damage from old strokes can cause irritable foci in the brain)?

The physical examination is essentially the same as outlined in earlier parts of this chapter. A thorough neurological evaluation also should be conducted as described above. Particular attention, however, should be paid to:

- Signs of head trauma, injury to the tongue, or injury to other parts of the body sustained during a seizure.
- Evidence of alcohol or drug abuse such as alcohol on the breath or needle tracks on the arms.
- Irregularities in heart rhythm. The patient should be monitored if these are found.

Treatment of an isolated seizure is aimed at maintaining an airway and preventing patient injury. The paramedic should use the following guidelines in managing seizures:

- Never restrain the patient during the tonic clonic phase of the seizure. Protect the patient from falling or banging into surrounding objects; clear furniture and other objects away from the patient. If possible, keep the patient on his or her side to reduce the possibility of aspiration.
- The use of a bite block or padded tongue blade is usually unnecessary. If the teeth are not already clenched, however, place a soft, gauze-wrapped tongue depressor between the molars to prevent tongue biting. Never jam any object into the mouth if the teeth are already clenched, as this can seriously injure the teeth and mouth. If possible, remove dentures, but be careful to avoid getting bitten.
- Maintain an airway, and administer oxygen.
- After the tonic clonic phase is over, make sure the patient is on his or her side and continue administering oxygen. Suction the patient's mouth if suction equipment is available.
- Keep the patient in a quiet, reassuring atmosphere. Avoid tight restraints, which may frighten patients and make them combative.
- Place the patient in a lying-down position for transport. Administer oxygen en route.

Status epilepticus is defined as two or more seizures without an intervening period of consciousness. Unlike an isolated seizure, status epilepticus is a major emergency. Repeated uncontrolled seizures may lead to aspiration, brain damage, fracture of the long bones and spine, cardiac muscle necrosis, and severe dehydration. In adults, the most common cause of status epilepticus is failure to take prescribed medicines. Treatment is aimed at maintaining the airway, preventing injury, and stopping the seizures. To do this, the paramedic should:

- Place the patient on the floor or a bed away from furniture. Never attempt to restrain the patient.
- Clear and maintain the airway. A nasopharyngeal airway may be helpful.
- Administer oxygen and assist ventilation if there are periods of hypoventilation or apnea. Hypoxia due to impaired respiration is a major complication of status epilepticus.
- Start an IV with D5W, simultaneously drawing blood for laboratory studies if possible. Secure the IV well.
- Obtain an order to administer 25 g of glucose IV.
- Administer diazepam (Valium) IV if the physician orders it due to difficulties in controlling the seizure. This drug must be administered cautiously because it can cause hypotension and apnea. Before administering diazepam, check the blood pressure. Inject 0.5 ml slowly, checking the blood pressure after each 0.5 ml. If the blood pressure begins to fall, stop injecting the drug and notify the physician. If 10 milligrams (mg) (2 ml) of diazepam do not stop the seizures, transport the patient immediately to the hospital. Continue to maintain the airway, administer oxygen, and keep the patient from hurting himself or herself while in transit.

Stroke

Stroke, also called cerebrovascular accident (CVA), is the common term for a sudden vascular catastrophe caused by thrombosis, embolus, or hemorrhage in the brain. When a blood clot blocks the artery carrying blood to a specific area of the brain, the functions governed by that area are damaged or lost. The exact symptoms of a stroke will depend on which area is damaged; motor centers, speech centers, and sensory centers in the brain are commonly affected. Thus, symptoms of stroke often include weakness, paralysis, speech disorders, confusion, and, in severe cases, coma.

Predisposing factors for strokes include high blood pressure (hypertension), diabetes, and abnormal blood lipid levels. Strokes commonly occur in elderly patients. Rare exceptions to this rule are young women taking oral contraceptives and young blacks with sickle-cell disease; both groups have increased susceptibility to cerebral embolism. Certain cardiac arrhythmias also can lead to stroke, either by decreasing cerebral blood flow or by dislodging emboli that can end up in the cerebral circulation.

Some patients experience transient ischemic attacks (TIA's), small strokes from which they recover completely within 12 hours. The symptoms of TIA's-weakness, paralysis, find speech disorders-are the same as those of strokes, but they are transient, lasting from a few seconds up to 12 hours. Many patients who have TIA's eventually suffer a complete stroke.

If a patient with suspected stroke is able to give a history, ask about any previous neurological symptoms that might have been TIA's. The EMT-P should determine the answers to these questions:

- Does the patient have a history of hypertension, cardiac disease, diabetes, sickle-cell disease, or previous stroke?

- If the patient is a woman, is she taking oral contraceptives?
- What symptoms did the patient notice first? Have the symptoms progressed?
- Did anything seem to precipitate the symptoms?
- Did the patient experience dizziness or palpitations? These symptoms may point to underlying cardiac disease as a cause of the stroke.
- Is the patient left or right handed?

On physical examination, the signs of stroke may be obvious or subtle. These signs include the following:

- Hemiparesis (weakness on one side of the body) or hemiplegia (paralysis on one side of the body). Occasionally only an arm or a leg may be affected.
- Speech disturbances that may vary from slurred speech (dysarthria), inability to speak at all (motor aphasia), inability to understand speech (receptive aphasia), to difficulty in naming objects. In the patient who is unable to speak, it is important to determine whether the patient can understand the paramedic. To test this, the patient can be given a simple command, such as "squeeze my hand."
- Headache.
- Confusion.
- Staggering gait or incoordination of fine motor movements.
- Visual disturbances.
- Inappropriate affect, with excessive laughing or crying.
- Coma, in massive stroke.

Paramedics should suspect stroke in any older patient who presents sudden confusion. The classic signs of stroke may not be present in each patient.

The neurological examination as described earlier should be performed on each patient with suspected stroke. Particular attention should be paid to the patient's speech, ability to follow commands, and ability to move the limbs.

Management of the patient with stroke is supportive and is aimed at trying to improve the blood flow and oxygenation to the brain. The paramedic should:

- Keep the patient flat
- Establish and maintain an airway
- Administer low-flow oxygen
- Monitor on telemetry or a portable unit, looking for cardiac arrhythmias
- If the patient is comatose or has significant arrhythmias, start an IV with D5W

A stroke can be frightening to an alert patient, especially if the ability to speak and communicate distress is lost. Paramedics should indicate they understand that the patient is going through a frightening experience. Each step of the evaluation and treatment should be explained, and paramedics should try to be as reassuring as possible.

Unit 4. Techniques of Management

Spinal Immobilization

The most common cause of spinal injury is trauma suffered during automobile accidents. The goal with the injured patient in an automobile is to remove the patient from the vehicle without further damaging the spinal cord. This is best accomplished by using both the short and long spine boards according to the following procedure:

- The first rescuer gets behind the patient, in the back seat if possible (assuming the patient is in front), and maintains axial traction to support the patient's neck in neutral position.
- The second rescuer can then apply a cervical collar to the patient's neck.
- The second rescuer next prepares a short spine board by placing the straps through the four side slots (not shown in figure).
- While the first rescuer continues to maintain axial traction, the second rescuer slides the short spine board behind the patient such that the patient's head is lined up with the head extension on the board. If the seat is curved, the paramedic may need to move the patient slightly forward to get the board behind the patient. Rescuers should coordinate their movements to maintain axial traction.
- When the short board is in position, a folded towel or an airsplint can be used to fill in the gap between the patient's neck and the board. The airsplint has the advantage that its size may be adjusted to fit each patient individually.
- The torso should then be strapped to the spine board using straps with quick release buckles first (straps must be taped to prevent inadvertant release). The straps also should be adjusted so that the buckles are high on the chest near the shoulders; buckles placed over the midchest will get in the way if cardiopulmonary resuscitation becomes necessary.
- The second rescuer then secures the patient's head to the board with a self-adhering (Kling) bandage. The rescuer should be careful not to cover the patient's mouth or to fasten the straps so tightly that the patient cannot open the mouth to cough or vomit.
- After the patient is securely strapped to the short spine board, the paramedic can remove the patient from the vehicle. The safest way to accomplish this is to rotate the patient carefully and slide him or her onto a long spine board. The long board should be positioned so that one end is resting firmly on the seat and the other end is held parallel to the ground. The patient should be carefully lowered into a supine position and slid gently along the long board. The paramedic will need to loosen the straps on the short board momentarily to lower the patient's legs.
- The patient should be lifted out of the vehicle by two rescuers, one holding the patient's trunk and another supporting the patient at the underarms. A patient should never be lifted by pulling up on the short spine board.

Patients injured in different types of accidents require different measures for extrication and spinal immobilization, but the basic principles are the same. The patient injured in a diving accident, for example, often has a cervical spine injury and must be approached with that possibility in mind. If the patient is still in the water, the procedure is as follows:

- The patient should be approached from the vertex. The first rescuer should place one arm under the patient's body such that the patient's head is supported on the rescuer's arm, and the patient's chest is supported on the rescuer's hand. The rescuer should place

the other arm across the patient's head and back, thus splinting the patient's head and neck between the rescuer's arms.
- The patient should be smoothly turned into the supine position while support is maintained on the head and neck. If the patient is not breathing, the rescuer should begin mouth-to-mouth resuscitation immediately, while the patient is still in the water.
- A rigid device-such as a wooden spine board, surfboard, door, or wooden plank-should be slid under the patient's head and neck. A cervical collar or other device can then be applied to further stabilize the neck.
- The board should then be floated to the edge of the water and lifted out. One rescuer should stabilize the patient on the board to prevent undue motion.
- After the board is removed from the water, the patient should be fastened to it with straps. An inflatable splint can be passed gently behind the patient's neck and inflated to serve as a neck roll. The patient should then be stabilized with roller bandages or sandbags.

Monitoring Patient Status

As noted earlier, the key to assessment-of patients with CMS problems is repeated observation. Such observation is easier and more accurate if the EMT-P uses a checklist that charts neurologic signs over time. The paramedic may want to use a checklist other than that developed by the American College of Surgeons. However, some type of form should be used to record repeated observations of the patient's neurological function.

GLOSSARY

<u>aura:</u> A premonitory sensation of impending illness; usually a word used in connection with an epileptic attack.
<u>Battle's sign:</u> Ecchymosis above the mastoid process indicating a basilar skull fracture.
<u>central neurogenic hyperventilation:</u> An abnormal pattern of ventilation seen in severe illness or injury involving the brain; characterized by marked tachypnea and hyperpnea.
<u>cerebellum:</u> That portion of the brain behind and below the cortex; its general function is the coordination of movement.
<u>cerebrum:</u> The main portion of the brain, occupying the upper and anterior part of the cranial cavity; site of voluntary motor control, the conscious will, and the emotions.
<u>Cheyne-Stokes respiration:</u> An abnormal breathing pattern, characterized by rhythmic waxing and waning of the depth of respiration, with regularly recurring periods of apnea; seen in association with central nervous system dysfunction.
<u>clonic:</u> Pertaining to the rapid contraction and relaxation of a muscle or group of muscles, cranium: The skull.
<u>doll's eye:</u> The phenomenon in which the eyes of an unconscious person move in the direction opposite to that in which the head is turned.
<u>dysarthria:</u> A defective speech pattern due to impairment of the tongue or other muscles needed for speech.
<u>extraocular movements:</u> The movements of the eye.
<u>focal motor seizure:</u> A seizure that is usually limited to one side of the body or one body part such as an arm.
<u>grand mal seizure:</u> A generalized motor seizure characterized by loss of consciousness; tonic clonic movements; and, sometimes, tongue biting, incontinence, and mental confusion.
<u>hemiparesis:</u> A weakness on one side of the body.
<u>hemiplegia:</u> A paralysis of one side of the body, idiopathic: Of unknown cause.
<u>medulla oblongata:</u> The portion of the brain between the cerebellum and spinal cord that contains the centers for control of respiration and heart beat.
<u>motor aphasia:</u> The inability to coordinate the muscles involved in speech; caused by damage to the brain center that controls speech (Broca's area).
<u>paralysis:</u> A loss of motor function.
<u>paraplegia:</u> The loss of both motion and sensation in the lower part of the body, most commonly due to damage to the spinal cord.
<u>petit mal seizure:</u> A type of epileptic attack; characterized by a momentary loss of awareness that is not accompanied by a loss of motor tone.
<u>postictal:</u> Referring to the period following the convulsive stage of a seizure.
<u>psychomotor seizure:</u> A seizure characterized by an altered personality state; in some patients, psychomotor seizures result in unexplained attacks of rage or stereotyped behavior.
<u>quadriplegia:</u> A paralysis of both arms and legs.
<u>raccoon sign:</u> The bilateral, symmetrical, periorbital ecchymosis seen with skull fracture; also called "coon's eyes."
<u>sensory aphasia:</u> The inability to understand spoken or written words depending on which word center is dysfunctional.
<u>status epilepticus:</u> The occurrence of two or more seizures without a period of complete consciousness between them.

sympathetic nervous system: A subdivision of the autonomic nervous system that governs the body's "fight or flight" reactions and stimulates cardiac activity.
tonic: Pertaining to the period in a seizure in which the muscles contract and do not relax.
transient ischemic attack (TIA): A temporary condition in which the blood supply to the brain is interfered with; usually an indication of an impending stroke.

www.ingramcontent.com/pod-product-compliance
Lightning Source LLC
Chambersburg PA
CBHW081825300426
44116CB00014B/2489